EVERYDAY Exotic

the cookbook

EVERYDAY Exotic

the cookbook

ROGER MOOKING
& ALLAN MAGEE

whitecap

Whitecap Books is known for its expertise in the cookbook market, and has produced some of the most innovative and familiar titles found in kitchens across North America. Visit our website at www.whitecap.ca.

Publisher: Michael Burch

Edited by Lesley Cameron

Cover design by Michelle Furbacher

Interior design and typesetting by Setareh Ashrafologhalai

Food photography by Ben Sharp

Food styling by Claudia Bianchi

Photos of Roger by Geoff George

Printed in Canada

Library and Archives Canada Cataloguing in Publication

Mooking, Roger, 1973-

    Everyday exotic : the cookbook / Roger Mooking and Allan Magee.

Includes index.

ISBN 978-1-77050-064-8

    1. Cooking. 2. Cookbooks. I. Magee, Allan, 1959- II. Title.

TX714.M665 2011   641.5   C2011-902968-5

The publisher acknowledges the financial support of the Government of Canada through the Canada Book Fund (CBF) and the Province of British Columbia through the Book Publishing Tax Credit.

11 12 13 14 15 5 4 3 2 1

ENVIRONMENTAL BENEFITS STATEMENT

Whitecap Books Ltd saved the following resources by printing the pages of this book on chlorine free paper made with 10% post-consumer waste.

TREES	WATER	ENERGY	SOLID WASTE	GREENHOUSE GASES
16 FULLY GROWN	7,407 GALLONS	7 MILLION BTUs	469 POUNDS	1,642 POUNDS

Environmental impact estimates were made using the Environmental Paper Network Paper Calculator. For more information visit www.papercalculator.org.

From Roger

To my grandparents and grandparents-in-law who blessed my family and me with their homespun magic for so many years. You inspire us to continue to pass along the blessings you showed us before you chose to watch over us—Moses, Ruby, Lio, Ames, Minnie, Charles, Blanche, Fred. To my parents and parents-in-law for teaching that food is love—Alloy, Gemma, Eleanor and Ed. Miles, everything I do, I do for you.

From Al

To Melanie, and Jake, John, Joseph and Stephen for all your love and inspiration.

CONTENTS

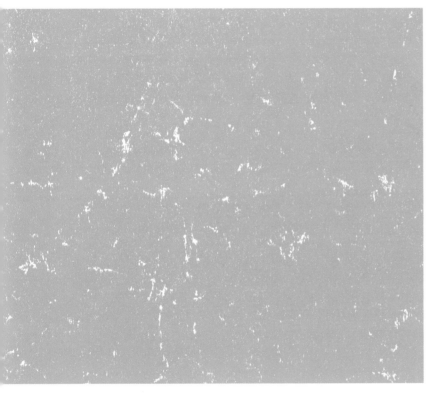

Introduction

Finally, it is here. An unusual number of folks have approached me on the street in the last while to ask that there be a cookbook of the television series *Everyday Exotic*. It has been in the womb and stubbornly long overdue but hopefully that only makes its birth more welcome. This is my Dr. Dre "Detox" album. Like the old Trinidadian adage says, "Water will find its own level," meaning all things will unfold as they will in their own time. Finally the water has levelled.

The *Everyday Exotic* journey has been a very exciting one, filled with an incredible amount of learning, sharing, growth and inspiration from many, many people whom you will find in the Acknowledgments. One of those people is a man named Al Magee, who has played a pivotal role as both co-creator and champion of the cause in so many unbelievable ways as well as being the person to name the show.

When I was five years old my family moved from Trinidad and Tobago to Edmonton, Alberta. Why, I'm still not sure. On one of my very first days in school one of my teachers patted me on the head and said, "My, aren't you exotic?" I believed I knew what the word "exotic" meant at that time but to this day it confuses me more than it did then. I do remember thinking, "Why is this woman patting me like a dog?" with a mix of what I recognize now as interest and fascination. But I also recognize now that at that time she may have never seen a person of colour in Alberta before, as I recall it being something of an event when we spotted another person of colour back then. I'm convinced she meant no harm or ill intent but that moment has stuck with me as noteworthy to this day.

I tell this story because it shows that our relationships with words, emotions and people are framed by every individual's own unique perspective. To her, I was "exotic" but approachable. To me, I was simply the same as the people I grew up with. The word "exotic" has crept in and out of my life over and over and here I am, once again known as the exotic guy, albeit with less head-patting. I'm still not sure what "exotic" really means. It's one of those fluid terms whose meaning changes according to who is speaking. As a wise man once said, one person's exotic is another person's everyday. One thing I am sure of, though, is that we shouldn't confuse "exotic" with "intimidating."

When I travel to Southeast Asia people I meet are inspired that I use their familiar spice powder for a hamburger—the hamburger being the "exotic" in this case. When I speak with my family in the Caribbean they are inspired that I have taken their beloved okra and made a chili with it, or deep-fried it with cornmeal. It is new while being familiar at the same time. For me, this is the essence of the *Everday Exotic* mystique. I believe the series enjoys great success in many parts of the world because food allows us to bridge the gaps in relating to one another from the familiar comforts of our own homes. Experimenting with other cultures' foods gives us an insight into those cultures, and gives us a tangible appreciation of what other cultures have to offer. We can venture to be "exotic" without fear of putting our foot in our mouth, whether your exotic is a hamburger or five-spice powder. We extend our comfort zone while remaining fully immersed in it; it is a culinary adventure. The next step is to share your food and experiences with others. This has silently been my motivation all along and the food allows me a tool to bridge the perceived cultural canyon without ever having to speak it.

Food is love. Spread love.

—*Roger Mooking*

Al Magee here. I count myself very fortunate to have had the *Everyday Exotic* experience and to have been able to work with and befriend Roger Mooking. We spent a year getting to know each other and trying out numerous ideas before we hit on the concept for *Everyday Exotic*. Since then we've produced 52 episodes of television that I'm very proud of and this cookbook. If we've done our jobs right, we'll have created a little bit more understanding and a little bit more acceptance in the world. I've been struggling to articulate our goals for the *Everyday Exotic* project but I think Roger nailed it when he said, "whether your exotic is a hamburger or five-spice powder." One person's exotic is another person's everyday, and the more we embrace each other's exotic, the more everyday it all becomes. That's been our vision for this project—and our vision for our lives.

Diversity is perfection.

—*Al Magee*

The Obedient Ingredient

When we were looking to name the *Everyday Exotic* television series, Al Magee assembled the team in one room with a blank whiteboard and had us each suggest 10 potential names. Obedient Ingredient was one of the names that popped up and although we obviously didn't use it as the name of the show, Al suggested that we use it during the show to explain one of the main elements, the ingredient. "Today's ingredient" just didn't have anything memorable enough for our liking and it didn't express what we were trying to achieve by introducing ingredients that many people find intimidating.

The notion behind the Obedient Ingredient is that the ingredient that was once out of reach becomes obedient once you learn how to master it. The ingredient intimidation melts away as you discover how to shop for it, what it looks like, where to find it and, finally, how to cook it several ways. In a a short time, something that was once beyond you is now readily embraced and subordinate. The Obedient Ingredient was born.

In this book the Obedient Ingredient is the star of each recipe while still being . . . well . . . obedient. It's a fun way of defining each meal. And it rhymes. And I'm a rapper. And sometimes it's just that simple.

—*Roger*

How to Build an *Everyday Exotic* Pantry

Here is a hit list of the ingredients, tools and equipment that have stood the test of time in my many and varied kitchens. Let's start with the good stuff—after all, where would our meals be without quality ingredients?

Staple Ingredients

Of course, I recommend you run out and buy every Obedient Ingredient featured in this book but they're not all staple pantry items. Run out and buy the perishables as you need them but make sure you are always stocked with the following goodies.

KOSHER SALT I love the subtle savoury lift that comes with this salt. It works to boost all the flavours you are seasoning before they turn too salty. The large, light granules also make it easy to see how much you are adding, so when you're seasoning a dish you can make sure you haven't missed a single corner and all the parts will be deeply flavoured. You can still add too much, but it is a bit more forgiving. Throughout this book, wherever you see the word salt I mean kosher salt unless specified otherwise. If you are using table salt or sea

salt my suggestion is to cut the quantity of salt in half as kosher salt is less "salty" than either sea or table salt. Also, feel free to season to taste where desired.

WHOLE BLACK PEPPERCORNS I never buy pre-ground black pepper. It has been ground months ago, stored in some vat somewhere, then packaged and put on a grocery store shelf where it sits until someone buys it (not me!), then it sits in a pantry until it's used up. Quite a journey. All the while the flavours are diminishing by the second and the bright peppery pop you were hoping for ends up being a poop. Not good. Always buy whole peppercorns and crush them the second you are ready to add them to your dish. They will release their essence and stay bright with flavour until you eat the food they're flavouring. That is goodness.

HONEY Call me crazy, but my cupboards at home have about six different kinds of honey at all times. It's quite surprising how distinct each one is, despite their shared round sweetness. The farmers' markets always seem to have a couple of honey purveyors to pick from and they are usually happy to let you know when their honey was bottled. Experiment with a couple of drops of honey in some savoury dishes as well as sweet ones—you'll be surprised at how much of a boost a couple of drops of this magic syrup will add to your dish. I love to add a bit of honey to vinaigrettes, sauces and stews; not so much to add sweetness as to help pull all the flavours together. Each different type of honey has its own distinct characteristic and I will often use different types of honey for experiment's sake in a recipe I make often. It's all about constantly experimenting. Throughout this cookbook you will see honey in the ingredients lists without specifying a particular type. This is to leave room for your own personal exploration. Have fun with it.

MEAT BONES This is not my inner taxidermist coming out. It's the poor college student/chef/waste controller in me. Every time I roast a chicken at home, or do a beef rib roast or bake a ham, you'll find me scraping the meat off the bones and bagging them up for the freezer. Once I have enough chicken bones to half-fill a stockpot I'll add them to carrots, celery, bay leaves, peppercorns and onions and make a bang-up chicken stock. Beef bones get the same treatment but sometimes they end up as demi-glace, the dark, rich sauce you get in restaurants that is so damn yummy. Those magical pork bones will be added to soups and stews to add that rich, sweet, meaty flavour that can only come from the oinker. Pork is my friend.

As well as the goodies I mentioned above, keep the following the staple pantry items in your cupboard:
- elbow macaroni
- balsamic vinegar
- five-spice powder
- cajun spice mix (see recipe, page 30)
- bay leaf
- rice of various types
- vegetable oil
- olive oil
- soy sauce

Keep some other staple pantry items in the fridge:
- hot sauce of various types (store for up to two months once opened)
- cilantro pesto (see recipe page 13) (store for up to one week)
- tomato chutney (see recipe page 13) (store for up to one week)
- ginger (store for up to one week or as long as it remains very firm)
- fresh limes (store for up to one week)
- fresh lemons (store for up to one week)

Finally, it's a good idea to have some ready-made pizza dough on hand (see recipe page 19). You can store it in the freezer, in a plastic bag with as much air removed as possible, for up to two weeks.

Partner Recipes

Most of the recipes in the first chapters of this book are set out as complete meals—main dish and side dishes, with accompanying dishes such as sauces, garnishes, relishes and so on. The accompanying dishes are so versatile. They can be used however you like—as a relish on a main dish, as a spread on a sandwich, as a way to bring new life to an old soup recipe of your own.

For this reason, I've highlighted the recipes for accompaniments in red in the book, for quick reference. I hope that you will be inspired to try something new with them yourself. Sometimes inspiration comes from the most humble of places; maybe you will find these partner recipes to be one of those places.

Tools and Equipment

There are so many kitchen tools on the market and I've been known to collect a fair number of them. As clutter slowly creeps in and takes over usefulness I end up giving away stuff I've barely used. If you have ever received a kitchen tool from me for a gift, now you know my guilty secret. The following, however, are indispensible:

HANDS My hands can become a meat mallet, a kneading hook, a whisk, a scraper, tongs, a strainer, or whatever I need at any given moment. With a bit of ingenuity and a distaste for washing dishes, you'll find that your hands will become your premium kitchen utensil. The best part is that they're free.

MORTAR AND PESTLE This goes back to those black peppercorns. Pepper mills are cool but with a mortar and pestle you can control the size of the grind. Sometimes a recipe calls for pepper to be cracked and other times to be ground. The mortar and pestle will do the trick and you can smell the love as you bash away. Pestos, aiolis and pastes are great to bang away at in the mortar as well. Again, the beauty is that you can see the size of the stuff you're breaking up and if you need to add a little more of something just drop it in and keep on going. The truth is, I like to bang around and make noise; this tool allows me to do just that. Cooking is making music and banging around creates a beat. I love a beat.

A SHARP KNIFE My basic knife list would include a chef's knife, paring knife, bread knife and cleaver. I use my chef's knife as my go-to tool for most tasks. The paring knife is to get into those stubborn little crevices, and the bread knife is so that you don't mangle that loaf of bread the baker made so lovingly. The cleaver is also a great day-to-day knife if you're accustomed to using it. I like to use it to break down stubborn bones and to split the backs out of chickens, for example. A sharp knife is safer than a dull knife any day and will actually cut you less often. Why? When you use a dull knife, stuff slips around the cutting board and you have to exert extra force to cut through whatever you are trying to cut. Extra force and slipping are not good when you're handling sharp objects. A good, sharp knife will allow you to apply just the right amount of force to accomplish the task at hand with less chance of slipping, so it's safer. My suggestion is always to buy the best knife that you can afford and a good tool for keeping it sharp. I'm lucky to have been taught how to sharpen my blades properly but you can find places that will do it for you if you don't have the proper training and you don't want to ruin your edge. One good knife will last you a couple of generations if you treat it properly, so it's a very good long-term purchase.

POTS AND PANS I work from the rule taught to me by my grandfather. He would always say, "Good things no cheap, cheap things no good." This was a man raised in a poor village in China's Guangdong province. He lived to be a centenarian, and his words resonate to this day. He would do without and save until he had enough for the thing that would last him a lifetime. Sometimes the doing without seemed never-ending, though.

Pots and pans are so different and the process of choosing the right one for your needs can be overwhelming. Copper, stainless, Teflon, ceramic, heavy gauge, light gauge, plastic handle, riveted handle—it's all a bit much. The pots I have now will surely make it to see my kids cook in them in their own homes. There will have been thousands of meals cooked in them and the good *chi* (energy) built up in them over time will guarantee a good meal comes out. Moses Mooking knew what he was talking about.

In North America, consumers covet a heavyweight pan with rivets, believing heavier is better and that the rivets suggest European excellence. In some Asian countries consumers look for smaller, lightweight products due to the restrictions of space in most households, as well the desire to toss the food in the pan, which is easier in a lighter-weight pan. Stainless steel is a great conductor of even heat and generally the thicker the steel the longer the pots will last and the more true the heat transference. It is not uncommon for manufacturers in North America to apply a thin coating of stainless steel to a heavier material to achieve the weight that is coveted. It is an illusion of excellence in many cases, as these heavier materials are often worse conductors of heat and distribute the heat unevenly. One of the best conductors of heat is aluminum, although it is very lightweight. The issue with aluminum products is that with repeated use they conduct the heat so surely that the aluminum softens and the product begins to warp. The benefit of aluminum products is that they are often inexpensive. It is a balancing act of your needs, your desires and your budgetary restrictions—as with most things in life.

These are some of my favourite North American "comfort foods." They are classic, familiar foods with hearty, filling, satisfying flavours and textures. They may not always be the healthiest foods for us, but, as my grandmother would say, "All things in moderation."

Comfort food has taken off in North American restaurants. It is appearing on the menus of the most upscale of restaurants to those dedicated to the craftiest burger, the artisanal pizza and the most decadent of mac and cheeses.

Instead of ordering takeout, stopping by a fast food joint or opening a box with an envelope of premixed ingredients, make your favourites from scratch with fresh ingredients. The heart loves cooking from scratch and the body loves the freshest of fresh ingredients.

COMFORT CLASSICS

OBEDIENT INGREDIENT

Five-Spice Powder

FIVE-SPICE LAMB BURGERS *with* HOMEMADE PICKLED CUCUMBER RELISH & QUICK FIVE-SPICE MAYO *served with* GRILLED CORN & CRISPY ONIONS

Serves 4

The distinguished flavour of this menu comes from the mix of five-spice powder and lime.

The **cucumber relish** offers a fresh alternative to the jarred variety. It will only take you five minutes and you'll make your guests feel special by serving a fresh homemade relish. And the **quick five-spice mayo** really brings out the flavour of the burger. Simply add the spice mix and a bit of lime juice to some mayonnaise and chill until you're ready to use. A versatile ingredient, this mayo is great on a sandwich or as a base for a slaw.

For a nice fresh side, try the **grilled corn**, which is inspired by Indian-style grilled corn and finished with a bit of lime and a sprinkle of the five-spice mix. You can grill the corn as you grill the burger.

And finally, we're used to having french fries or onion rings with our burger, but both can be heavy and greasy and the rings are often too doughy. These light, **crispy onions** provide the crispy crunch that we want with our burger with a fraction of the calories and even more of the full flavour of the onions. Fry them up, dust them with five-spice powder and salt and eat them with your fingers—the way they should be eaten.

Five-Spice Lamb Burgers

PATTIES

2 lb (1 kg) ground lamb

1 shallot, minced

1 garlic clove, minced

1 egg yolk

1 Tbsp (15 mL) five-spice powder

½ Tbsp (7.5 mL) minced ginger

Salt

Pepper

TO SERVE

4 buns

Quick Five-Spice Mayo

Cucumber Relish

1 ripe tomato, sliced

Place all the patty ingredients in a bowl and mix well. Using your hands, make four 8 oz (230 g) burgers. Place the burgers in the fridge for 1 hour to allow the flavours to infuse.

Heat the grill to medium heat. Grill the burgers until cooked through.

Toast the buns on the grill. Assemble the burgers with the five-spice mayo, pickled cucumber relish and sliced tomato.

Cucumber Relish

1 tsp (5 mL) coriander seeds

1 Tbsp (15 mL) vegetable oil

½ red onion, finely diced

1 red finger chili, seeded and diced

¼ cup (60 mL) white wine vinegar

¼ cup (60 mL) sugar

1 English cucumber, seeded and diced

Salt

½ bunch mint leaves, coarsely chopped

In a sauté pan, toast the coriander seeds over medium to high heat. Add the oil and sweat the red onion until translucent. Add the diced chili and stir. Stir in the white wine vinegar and the sugar and allow the sugar to dissolve. Add the cucumber

and cook for 5 to 7 minutes over medium heat to reduce slightly and to get a lightly glazed consistency.

Season with salt and cool. Add the mint and toss to incorporate.

Store in an airtight container refrigerated for up to one week.

Quick Five-Spice Mayo

½ cup (125 mL) mayonnaise

Juice of 1 lime

2 tsp (10 mL) five-spice powder

In a small bowl, mix the mayonnaise, lime juice and five-spice powder. Refrigerate until ready to use.

Store in an airtight container refrigerated for up to two weeks.

Crispy Five-Spice Onions

2 sweet onions, cut in half and sliced
    thinly on a mandolin

8 cups vegetable oil, for frying

¼–½ cup (60–125 mL) cornstarch

½ tsp (2.5 mL) five-spice powder

½ tsp (2.5 mL) kosher salt

Soak the sliced onion in cold water for 10 minutes.

In a large, wide-bottomed pot, heat the vegetable oil to 325°F (160°C) (160°C). Line a tray with paper towels. Drain the onions, dry them well in a kitchen towel, then dredge them lightly in the cornstarch and deep-fry in batches. Move the onions around while frying to prevent clumping. Remove the onions from the oil just before they turn brown and place them on a serving tray lined with paper towel; they will continue to colour on the tray. Season the rings with five-spice powder and salt while they are still hot and glistening with oil. Eat them the way they should be eaten: with your fingers!

Grilled Five-Spice Corn with Lime

4 fresh cobs of corn, husked

2 limes cut in half

1 Tbsp (15 mL) five-spice powder

Salt

Heat the grill to medium heat to get a bit of char on the corn. Place the cobs of corn on the grill unt il cooked through and charred, turning every 2 or 3 minutes for approximately 15 minutes. Rub the corn with the lime, then season with the five-spice powder and salt. Serve immediately while still hot.

" Most people love a good burger and I love to make mine with lamb. Sometimes I don't tell people that I've included five-spice powder in the burger so I can enjoy the look of surprise and delight on their faces when they taste the spice with the lamb. I do a lot of cooking demos and I love to serve this lamb burger in a bite-sized version. The audience goes nuts for them.

OBEDIENT INGREDIENTS

Cilantro & Coriander

CORIANDER MEATLOAF *with* CILANTRO PESTO & TOMATO CHUTNEY *served with* GRILLED ZUCCHINI & ONIONS

Serves 4

This **coriander meatloaf** combines both ground beef and ground pork, picking up on a worldly tradition of combining meats for more flavour. We see it in Italy and in the Philippines in the preparation of meatballs. The sweetness of the pork combines nicely here with the richness of the beef. Of course, if you don't like one or the other, leave it out and add more of the ground meat that you do prefer. If you're going to use chicken, use ground chicken thighs. They're much juicier.

What makes this everyday meal exquisite is the combination of coriander and cilantro. What's the difference? They both come from the same plant. Cilantro is the leaves, stems and root of the coriander plant, and coriander is the

dried seeds. The seeds have a warm, nutty orange flavour. The leaves have a brighter citrus flavour. Not everyone likes the flavour. Some people love it. No way to find out but by trying.

I love the taste of roasted ground coriander seeds, and when combined with paprika, mustard and chopped cilantro leaves, it creates a one-of-a-kind flavour. In this menu, the cilantro in the tomato chutney and pesto echoes the coriander base in the meatloaf. The flavours of the tomato chutney and the cilantro pesto complement one another. Both score high on the versatility meter. You can use them with dumplings, chicken or fish, or toss them with a macaroni salad for extra flavour.

Tomato chutney is a red sauce textured with chunks of ripe tomato—a fresh take on ketchup. The brown sugar brings the sweet and the white wine vinegar brings the sour. The cilantro echoes the base of the meatloaf. Another great condiment is the cilantro pesto—just a bunch of ground-up cilantro blended into a paste that complements the sweet and sour of the chutney. It couldn't be any simpler.

The spicy full flavour of the meatloaf and the condiments needs a straight-up simple side: grilled zucchini and onions. These vegetables' whose natural flavours expand with just a bit of olive oil and freshly ground pepper.

Coriander Meatloaf

1 Tbsp (15 mL) butter
1 tsp (5 mL) olive oil
½ red onion, diced
3 cloves garlic, minced
2 eggs
⅓ cup (80 mL) 35% cream
1 Tbsp (15 mL) Dijon mustard
1½ lb (750 g) ground beef
1½ lb (750 g) ground pork
Salt
Pepper
2 Tbsp (30 mL) cilantro stems, finely chopped
1½ Tbsp (22.5 mL) coriander seeds, toasted and crushed in a mortar and pestle
1 tsp (5 mL) paprika

Preheat the oven to 350°F (175°C).

Heat the butter and olive oil in a sauté pan and sweat the onion and garlic over medium heat for approximately 5 minutes. In a large bowl, whisk the eggs, cream and Dijon mustard. Add the ground beef and pork to the bowl and season with salt and pepper. Add the onion mixture, cilantro stems, toasted coriander seeds and paprika to the bowl. Carefully fold the ingredients together. Do not overmix. Place the meatloaf mixture in a 9- × 5-inch (2 L) pan, tapping down to remove any air pockets.

Place the meatloaf pan inside a larger baking dish and pour water halfway up inside the larger dish. Bake the meatloaf in the water bath for 1½ hours.

Tomato Chutney

1 Tbsp (15 mL) olive oil
½ red onion, diced
1 clove garlic minced
1 green finger chili, split in half
6 plum tomatoes, with seeds, roughly chopped
Salt
2 Tbsp (30 mL) brown sugar
2 Tbsp (30 mL) white wine vinegar
1 Tbsp (15 mL) cilantro, chopped

In a pan, heat the olive oil over medium heat. Add the onion, garlic and chili and sauté until lightly caramelized. Add the tomatoes and season with salt. Turn the heat to medium-high. Stir in the brown sugar and vinegar. Cook for 5 to 10 minutes until the liquid has evaporated and the tomatoes have cooked down. Garnish with the cilantro. Serve a heaping spoonful with each slice of meatloaf.

Store in an airtight container refrigerated for up to one week.

Cilantro Pesto

1 bunch green onion tops, cut in half
1 bunch cilantro, roughly chopped
½ cup (125 mL) olive oil
2 Tbsp (30 mL) white wine vinegar
Salt

In a blender, place the green onion tops, cilantro, olive oil and vinegar. Season with salt and purée into a paste.

Store in an airtight container refrigerated for up to one week.

Grilled Zucchini and Onions

3 small zucchinis, cut in half lengthwise
1 sweet onion, cut into 4 rings
1 Tbsp (15 mL) olive oil
Salt
Pepper

Heat the grill to medium-high heat. Place the zucchinis and onion side by side on a tray, drizzle with olive oil and season with salt and pepper. Grill the zucchinis and onion until slightly softened, turn once, then remove.

> "When I was a kid I used to hang out at my friend Trevor's house. His family lived on meatloaf. I'd be there for dinner and for sure the next day at school Trevor would show up with bulging meatloaf sandwiches. I was envious—meatloaf has always been one of my favourite comfort foods. It's a great dish to experiment with because you really have to try hard to mess it up.

OBEDIENT INGREDIENT

Curry Powder

CURRIED MACARONI & CHEESE PIE

Serves 4

The love in this dish comes from the addition of **curry powder**, garlic, onion and green chili. In India, the birthplace of curry powder, the spice is referred to as masala. Every family makes their own blend of spices and, of course, each family believes that theirs is the best.

I like to start with elbow macaroni, cooked al dente. I pair it with provolone cheese, which has a mild, neutral taste that doesn't compete with any of the rich flavours I'll be adding. It's also nice and stringy once melted and that gives you a very cheesy, deliciously gooey pie. You can substitute any mild cheese, like mozzarella, but provolone is particularly gooey once melted.

Curried Macaroni and Cheese Pie

1¼ lb (625 g) elbow macaroni

2 Tbsp (30 mL) + 1 tsp (5 mL) vegetable
   oil

½ cup (125 mL) butter

½ red onion, diced

2 cloves garlic, diced

1 green chili, split lengthwise but kept in
   one piece, with seeds intact (optional)

¼ cup (60 mL) + 2 Tbsp (30 mL) all-
   purpose flour

1 Tbsp (15 mL) curry powder

5 cups (1.25 L) 2% milk

2½ cups (625 mL) shredded provolone
   cheese

½ cup (125 mL) breadcrumbs

1 bunch asparagus, bottoms trimmed

Salt

Bring a large pot of salted water to the boil. Add the macaroni and cook until al dente, 10 to 12 minutes. Drain and transfer to a large baking sheet. Drizzle with the 2 Tbsp (30 mL) vegetable oil and stir gently to prevent clumping. Allow to cool completely.

Preheat the oven to 350°F (175°C).

In a large pot, heat the butter and 1 tsp (5 mL) oil over medium heat. Add the onion, garlic and green chili and sauté until tender and translucent, approximately 2 minutes. Add the flour and curry powder to create a roux, whisking to remove any lumps as you cook the flour, approximately 1 minute. Then over low heat, add the milk slowly while whisking to create a curried creamy sauce. Bring the sauce to a simmer and continue to whisk for 2 minutes. Remove the sauce from the heat, remove the green chili, add 2 cups (500 mL) of the grated cheese and stir.

Stir the cooked macaroni into the curry sauce, mix and season with salt. Transfer the macaroni mixture into a 9- × 9-inch (2.5 L) baking dish. Sprinkle the top with ¼ cup (60 mL) of the bread-crumbs and ¼ cup (60 mL) of the cheese. Arrange the asparagus in a line over the breadcrumbs and cheese. Sprinkle the remaining breadcrumbs and cheese over the asparagus. Bake the curried macaroni and cheese in the oven for 30 to 40 minutes, until the top is golden brown.

"

In Trinidad I grew up on my family's macaroni pie, which we'd bake so it set, and serve it as a side dish on a special occasion. Caribbean food is always fresh and simple—nothing is ever prepared from a box. When I moved to North America I discovered a different kind of mac and cheese. It came in a box and the sauce was pastey and made from an orange powder. This recipe combines the North American preference for a rich and gooey mac and cheese with the Caribbean tradition of a baked and set pie.

Buffalo Mozzarella

BUFFALO MOZZARELLA & TOMATO PIZZA Serves 4

Buffalo mozzarella is extremely versatile and always best when it's as fresh as humanly possible. There are few things as satisfying as tearing open a still-warm ball of buffalo mozzarella.

I love the fresh mild flavour of buffalo mozzarella and the light taste of the **tomatoes**, but what I really love about this pizza is getting my hands into it: crushing the tomatoes by hand and tearing the mozzarella. Nothing connects us to our food more than getting right in it with our hands. The

dough itself uses a bit of white wine, which imparts a fully developed flavour that mimics a sour dough.

This is a great basic pizza to start your pizza making and you can easily add your favourite toppings to customize it. Or feel free to delete the toppings and use this dough recipe for making a focaccia bread. Roll out the dough to an even ¼-inch thickness, press your fingers in the dough to make dimples and drizzle with your best quality olive oil and fresh picked herbs before baking.

Pizza Dough

1¼ cups (310 mL) warm water

1 Tbsp (15 mL) sugar

One 8 g package (approximately 2¼ tsp/ 11 mL) instant yeast

3¼ cups (810 mL) all-purpose flour + extra for dusting

1 Tbsp (15 mL) salt

¼ cup (60 mL) dry white wine, room temperature

2 Tbsp (30 mL) + ½ tsp (2.5 mL) olive oil

Combine ¼ cup (60 mL) of the warm water with the sugar in a small bowl. Add the yeast and stir to dissolve, checking that bubbles start to form after a few minutes. If no bubbles form, you have to start over.

In the meantime, place the flour and salt in a large bowl (or food processor). Make a well in the centre of the dry ingredients and add the remaining 1 cup (250 mL) warm water, the wine and 2 Tbsp (30 mL) of the olive oil. (Or add the wet ingredients to the food processor.)

Once the yeast mixture is bubbling, use a wooden spoon to stir it into the dry ingredients until the dough comes together (or pulse the yeast mixture and the ingredients in the food processor). Lightly flour a work surface, turn the dough out and knead for approximately 5 minutes, until the dough is smooth and elastic.

Lightly oil a large bowl with ½ tsp (2.5 mL) of olive oil. Place the ball of the dough on top of the oil in the bowl, flip the dough over seam side down, cover with plastic wrap and place near a warm dry spot to rise until the dough has doubled in size, approximately 1 hour.

Remove the ball of dough from the bowl, punch it down to release any air, cover again with plastic wrap and reserve at room temperature for assembling pizzas if using immediately. Once you're ready to assemble the pizzas, split the dough into two equal portions (approximately 1 lb/450 g each). Each portion will make one large pizza.

If you only want to make one pizza, save the remaining dough in a clean, resealable plastic bag. Lightly oil the inside of the bag, remove as much air as possible, and store in the fridge for up to two days or in the freezer for up to three months. Thaw the frozen dough in the fridge overnight before use and sit at room temperature for 1 hour before using.

Store in the fridge for up to two days, or in the freezer for up to three months. Makes 2 lb (1 kg) dough.

Buffalo Mozzarella and Tomato Pizza

1 lb (500 g) Pizza Dough

Flour and cornmeal for dusting

1 cup (250 mL) whole canned tomatoes

1 ball buffalo mozzarella, drained from water

1 Tbsp (15 mL) olive oil

¼ cup (60 mL) basil, leaves torn

Place a pizza stone in the oven and preheat oven to 450°F (230°C). (If you don't have a pizza stone, use an inverted baking sheet large enough to hold the dough.)

Dust a clean, dry work surface with flour and roll out the pizza dough to ¼ inch (6 mm) thick. Dust a large cutting board or wooden pizza paddle with cornmeal and place the rolled dough on top. Dump the canned tomatoes into a large bowl, pick them up with your hands and gently squeeze out any excess liquid. Scatter the tomatoes over the pizza dough, leaving 1 inch (2.5 cm) clear around the edges of the crust. Tear pieces of buffalo mozzarella and place them on the pizza. Place the olive oil in a small bowl and brush the edges of the dough with it.

Lift the board with the pizza and slide the pizza onto the heated pizza stone in the oven. Bake the pizza until the crust is slightly golden and the cheese has melted, approximately 10 minutes.

Garnish the pizza with torn basil leaves, slice and serve.

"I recently found out that many of my friends do a weekly pizza night because it's an opportunity for the whole family to cook together and clean out the fridge. I was inspired by this to create a pizza that can be made at home midweek or, with a little bit of planning, any time you feel like pizza.

You start with the dough, which is best made ahead. Make it the night before or in the morning to give it time to rise.

Every Sunday I take my girls swimming. Before we leave I make a batch of pizza dough, and by the time we get back from the pool, the dough is ready and we all get busy picking our pizza toppings and making our pizza.

Many cultures build meals around some kind of meat or fish and starch: in Japan it's fish and rice; in China it's chicken and rice; in the Caribbean it's curried goat in a roti; in North America it's roast beef and potatoes. I want to go headlong into meat and potatoes from an everyday North American perspective while drawing inspiration from around the world.

MEAT, POTATOES & MORE

Camembert

BALSAMIC MARINATED ROAST BEEF *served with* MASHED POTATOES *&* SAUTÉED MUSHROOMS *&* BAKED CAMEMBERT *with* HERB OIL

Serves 4

Camembert is similar to brie in that it is a cheese with a rind, but it comes from different regions in France. It is easily obedient because of its mild flavour.

The **balsamic** marinade seasons the outer layer of the meat and penetrates it; when you slice it you'll see a dark ring around the edge. The balsamic also adds a beautiful sweet to the strong aromatic pine flavour of the rosemary and protects the savouriness of the meat. Vinegar and meat go together really well, as do herbs and meat, so this is the perfect combo.

Often where there is meat and potato there is a sauce, maybe gravy, ketchup, or a condiment like horseradish. I want to show you a different way to make a sauce using camembert cheese. It's actually faster than cooking down gravy and makes a special occasion meal seem very special. This meal really expresses the notion of creating sauces out of all sorts of ingredients. As for versatility, the **herb oil** can be tossed with spinach, zucchini, or rapini.

We take the camembert, open it up into two discs, stuff it with a bunch of herbs, pour on a bit of oil, seal it back up and let it get all hot and steamy as the cheese melts with the herbs, and then pour the herbed camembert onto the roast beef like a gravy.

The next thing you need is a good basic **mashed potato**. In this recipe, I haven't added any milk or cream because

continued

of the creamy cheese sauce that's served alongside; the butter and oil are enough.

Now all that's needed is a vegetable component. **Mushrooms** go well with roast beef and potatoes, and this recipe uses reserved herb oil from the sauce to toss them.

Balsamic Marinated Roast Beef

1 cup (250 mL) balsamic vinegar
5 cloves garlic, chopped
2 Tbsp (30 mL) black pepper
½ cup (125 mL) olive oil
¼ cup (60 mL) chopped rosemary
One 2½–3 lb (1.25–1.5 kg) eye of round
    (beef)

Place the balsamic vinegar, garlic and black pepper in a small sauté pan over medium to high heat. Reduce to two-thirds of the original volume, approximately 2 minutes. Remove the pan from the heat and stir in the olive oil and rosemary, allowing the mixture to cool.

Pour the balsamic marinade into a baking pan just large enough to hold the roast, then place the beef in the pan and coat it using your hands. Marinate in the fridge for a minimum of half an hour to a maximum of 24 hours.

When ready to cook, preheat the oven to 350°F (175°C) and remove the marinated beef from the fridge.

Cook the beef for 45 minutes to 1 hour, until it is medium-rare with an internal temperature of between 130°F (54°C) and 140°F (60°C). Remove the beef from the oven and allow it to rest in a tent of aluminum foil for 10 minutes before slicing.

Mashed Potatoes

3 lb (1.5 kg) Yukon gold potatoes
¼ cup (60 mL) butter
2 Tbsp (30 mL) olive oil
3 Tbsp (45 mL) reserved potato water
Salt to taste

Peel and quarter the potatoes and cook in heavily salted water until tender. Drain the potatoes, reserving 3 Tbsp (45 mL) of the water, and then place them back in the pot.

Mash or rice the potatoes, then fold in the butter, olive oil, reserved potato water and salt. Gently fold until the ingredients are incorporated, tasting and adjusting the seasoning, if necessary.

Baked Camembert and Herb Oil

One 8–10 oz (230–300 g) wheel of
    camembert
¼ cup (60 mL) olive oil
2 Tbsp (30 mL) thyme
2 Tbsp (30 mL) marjoram
1 Tbsp (15 mL) rosemary, chopped
1 tsp (5 mL) black pepper

Cut the camembert wheel in half as you would a layer cake, using a sharp knife that has been run under hot water. Set aside.

Preheat the oven to 350°F (175°C) and line a baking dish, or ovenproof sauté pan, with parchment paper.

Place all the ingredients, except the camembert, in a bowl and mix to incorporate. Place the bottom half of the camembert in the lined dish. Spoon 1 Tbsp (15 mL) of the herb oil in the centre of the camembert. Place the top half of the Camembert on and pour 1 Tbsp (15 mL) of the herb oil overtop. Bake in

the oven until the camembert has melted, approximately 10 minutes.

Sautéed Mushrooms

2 Tbsp (30 mL) herb oil reserved from
    Baked Camembert
1 tsp (5 mL) butter
1 lb (500 g) cremini mushrooms,
    quartered
Salt
Pepper

Place the reserved herb oil and butter in a sauté pan over medium to high heat. Toss the cremini mushrooms in the pan and sauté until slightly caramelized. Season to taste with salt and pepper and remove from the heat.

To serve, place the roast beef and mashed potatoes on a plate, and spoon sautéed mushrooms and baked camembert overtop.

> " I love visiting my friends for special occasion meals. If you need to make a meat and potatoes meal to impress—or you're having me over for dinner—this is the recipe for you. I once worked at a catering company where the owner (Hi, Brenda!) roasted a tenderloin in balsamic vinegar, and I always loved it.

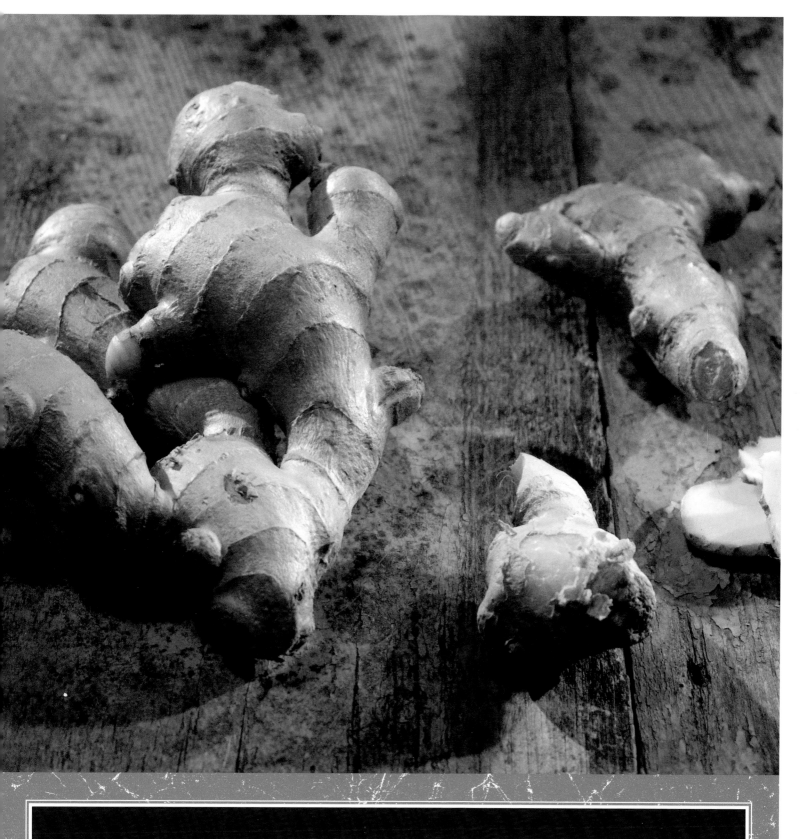

OBEDIENT INGREDIENT

Ginger

GINGER POT ROAST *&* GINGER PINEAPPLE COMPOTE *served with* QUINOA SALAD

Serves 4

Braising is cooking something submerged in a liquid—usually between 225°F (105°C) and 325°F (160°C)—slowly, to break down the connective tissue. Sometimes in the kitchen you need a little bit of patience—with braising, you can enjoy the cooking time.

Set up the **ginger pot roast** and then leave it. Go relax, or do some chores. When you come back, dinner will be ready. You don't want to leave it for four hours or it will start to dry out, but two and a half to three hours is fine. Always cook this roast covered, for a nice steaming environment, so the liquid doesn't evaporate.

Ginger beer comes from the Caribbean. Made by fermenting ginger and sugar, it's gingery, spicy, mostly clear, very refreshing—in my opinion, more refreshing than beer on a hot day—and a great settler for an upset stomach.

Ginger is extremely adaptable in that it can be purchased in many forms—fresh ground, as a beverage, or crystallized. This recipe uses ginger beer as the braising liquid instead of a meat stock. Mix it with a chicken stock, and the sugar in the ginger beer will help to glaze the meat. Strain the liquid leftover from braising and reserve it to create a delish finish for the pot roast.

Leftovers make for a great pulled pork sandwich. Reheat the meat in some sauce and pile it on a bun. Heaven.

I like to serve the ginger pot roast with **quinoa salad**. It's such a substantial piece of meat that you'll want to pair it with a less substantial starch. Quinoa, the ancient grain from Egypt, is light, airy and so easy to cook. Just boil it.

The **ginger pineapple compote** is just cooked-down fruit. It's generally cooked longer to break it down (chutney is cooked less to reserve its texture). It's kind of like a relish on a hamburger.

Pork and pineapple is a classic combination (think ham and pineapple pizza): the sweet acid of the pineapple takes well to ginger and the spicy notes of the ginger play well off the pineapple. You can also add chilies to the compote to spice it up as a condiment any time you want a bit more heat.

Ginger Pot Roast

4 lb (1.8 kg) pork picnic shoulder, bone in
Salt
2 Tbsp (30 mL) vegetable oil
1 large onion, peeled and quartered
4 cloves garlic, smashed
2 Tbsp (30 mL) ginger, smashed
3 cinnamon sticks
2 bay leaves
1 Tbsp (15 mL) black peppercorns
1 Tbsp (15 mL) coriander seeds
1 Tbsp (15 mL) fennel seeds
½ tsp (2.5 mL) cumin
Two 12 oz (355 mL) bottles ginger beer
1–2 cups (250–500 mL) chicken stock
2 Tbsp (30 mL) molasses

Preheat the oven to 350°F (175°C).

Season the pork with salt. Heat the vegetable oil in a large ovenproof pot over high heat and sear the pork on all sides, approximately 7 to 10 minutes. Remove the pork and set it aside. Using the same pot, cook the onion, garlic and ginger over medium heat until lightly browned. Add all of the spices and toast until fragrant. Deglaze, by adding the ginger beer and the chicken stock gradually, scraping until all the browned bits are off the bottom of the pan. You may not need all the chicken stock. Stir in the molasses and bring the liquid up to a simmer. Add the pork, cover the pot with a lid and place it in the oven. Braise in the oven until the pork is tender (approximately

2½ hours). Turn the pork over halfway through cooking.

Once the pork is tender, remove it from the pot. Remove the fat cap and cut the meat into 2-inch pieces. Set aside. Using a fine strainer, pour the liquid into a large, wide pot. Over high heat, reduce the braising liquid by two-thirds until thick enough to coat the back of a spoon. Spoon the sauce over the pork to glaze before serving.

Quinoa Salad

1½ cups (375 mL) quinoa
½ bunch green onion
Zest and juice of 1 lemon
¼ cup (60 mL) extra virgin olive oil
1 tsp (5 mL) minced ginger
Salt
½ English cucumber, halved, seeds removed and diced
½ bunch fresh mint, roughly chopped

Cook the quinoa according to the package directions. Set aside.

Smash the whites of the green onions and slice finely. Chop the green tops. Put the white parts in a bowl with the lemon juice, zest, oil, ginger and salt to taste and stir to incorporate. In a large bowl, mix

the cooked quinoa, cucumber and the green onion tops. Add the white onion mixture to the quinoa mixture and gently toss. Add the mint. Gently toss and season to taste with salt.

Ginger Pineapple Compote

1 pineapple
2 Tbsp (30 mL) butter
1 Tbsp (15 mL) sugar
Salt
2 Tbsp (30 mL) minced ginger

Peel, core and finely dice the pineapple. Melt the butter in a sauté pan over medium heat. Add the pineapple, season with the sugar and salt to taste and sauté over medium heat for 5 minutes. There's no need to keep stirring as the sugar will dissolve and won't burn. Add the ginger, stir and remove from the heat. Serve warm or at room temperature.

Store in a clean, dry container in the fridge for up to three days. Makes 4 to 6 healthy portions.

Serve the pork on top of a bed of quinoa salad. The pineapple compote can be served on the side.

OBEDIENT INGREDIENT

Cajun Spice

CAJUN BLACKENED STEAK *served with* SUGAR SNAP PEAS

Serves 4

The secret to achieving the flavour is not just the heat of the pan but also the heat of the spice mix. Like a curry powder or masala mix, **Cajun spice mix** can be used for beef, chicken, pork, fish and even potatoes.

If you love a rib eye steak, get yourself a rib eye, but if you love a strip loin or a tenderloin, get yourself a T-bone so you get a bit of both. When you're cooking the meat on the bone, you get massive flavour. To take it a step further, submerge the T-bone in a root beer marinade for 24 hours. It will tenderize the meat and add sweetness, which offsets the heat of the spice mix that sears on when you blacken the steak. I like serving this one rare or medium rare. I served it at the Food Network Canada 10th Anniversary party to rave reviews.

To stay with the nod to the south make potato gumbo (see page 126). It's a sticky lip-smacking stew that's a great way to enjoy potato with your meat.

Sugar snap peas are a quick and tasty way to round out the meal. Blanch the peas and add a bit of salt. There is so much going on with the flavours of the steak, the spice mix, the dry sear and the root beer. The gumbo is also loaded with flavour, so you want to keep the vegetable basic. Even though you can do things to enhance a vegetable's flavour, sometimes it's best just to honour its straight-up taste and texture.

Cajun Spice Mix

2 Tbsp (30 mL) freshly ground pepper
1 Tbsp (15 mL) hot paprika
1 Tbsp (15 mL) sweet paprika
1 Tbsp (15 mL) garlic powder
1 Tbsp (15 mL) onion powder
1 Tbsp (15 mL) ground thyme
1 Tbsp (15 mL) filé powder (optional)
1 Tbsp (15 mL) mustard powder
1 tsp (5 mL) cayenne

Thoroughly mix all ingredients in a small bowl. Set aside.

Store in a clean, dry container in the pantry. Makes enough for 4 to 6 steak portions.

Cajun Blackened Steak

Four 2 lb (1 kg) T-bone steaks
4 cups (1 L) root beer
Cajun Spice Mix
2 Tbsp (30 mL) salt

Marinate the steaks in the root beer, covered, in the fridge for 24 hours for best results.

Place the Cajun spice mix on a tray. Remove the steaks from the root beer and pat dry with a paper towel. Heat a cast-iron pan over medium heat. Season the steaks with salt and press them one at a time into the Cajun spice mix. Place the steaks, one at a time, in the cast-iron pan and sear for approximately 2 to 3 minutes each side for a medium rare. Allow the steaks to rest, tented with aluminum foil, for 3 to 4 minutes before serving.

"Some good friends of mine in the music business took me to the Southern United States for a festival and introduced me to Southern flavours. Man, it changed my life. It was the first time I ever had blackened anything. Whether it was catfish, chicken or steak, I loved the blackened flavour. It's a flavour that defines the South.

Sugar Snap Peas

1 cup (250 mL) sugar snap peas
Kosher salt for boiling
1 tsp (5 mL) sea salt

Clean the snap peas. Bring a pot of water well salted with kosher salt to a boil. Boil the peas for 1 to 2 minutes, or until they turn bright green and still have some crunch, and then plunge them into an ice bath to stop them cooking.

Drain well through a colander and transfer to a serving dish. Garnish with the sea salt and serve hot.

Place the Cajun blackened steak on a plate and spoon the sugar snap peas over it. Garnish with flaked salt. For a complete meal, serve with Potato Gumbo (see page 126).

OBEDIENT INGREDIENT

Szechuan Peppercorn

SZECHUAN PEPPERCORN STEAK *served with* CREAMED SPINACH & SWEET POTATOES & GRILLED GREEN ONIONS

Serves 4

In classic French cuisine there is a dish called *steak au poivre*, which is cracked pepper packed on the side of a steak. It's very basic but it has stood the test of time as one of the very best ways to prepare a steak. Instead of just black peppercorns, I'm going to suggest you use **Szechuan peppercorns**. Before anesthesia, dentists would use Szechuan pepper to numb patients' mouths. We're not going for that effect here but you will experience a certain heat with a unique floral finish. By using one different ingredient you transform a traditional dish, one you already know and love, into a new classic.

Next, you'll use the same Szechuan peppercorns to glaze a simple, grilled **sweet potato**. When the sweet potatoes

are fully cooked, we take them out and glaze them. The glaze combines the sweetness of the brown sugar and the numbing spice of the Szechuan peppercorns.

Another standard side dish for steak is **creamed spinach**. It's a classic pairing that you will find in North America as standard fare in hotels and the best steak houses. We've given a bit of a kick to this classic with the addition of some chilies. It's a very simple, very delicious dish and you can serve it with any number of menus, including Ginger Pot Roast (page 27), Papaya Chicken (page 76) and even Daikon Soup (page 120). To add a flourish at the end, you're going to char some green onions.

Szechuan Peppercorn Spice Mix

3 Tbsp (45 mL) black peppercorns
3 Tbsp (45 mL) Szechuan peppercorns
2 Tbsp (30 mL) dried papaya seeds*
    (optional)

Place the black peppercorns in a mortar and pestle and grind. Add the Szechuan peppercorns and papaya seeds (if using) and grind again. Transfer the Szechuan peppercorn spice mix to a container.

Makes enough for 4 to 5 steak portions.

* I save the seeds and dry them whenever I open a papaya. If you don't have any, you could use 1 Tbsp (15 mL) each of black peppercorns and Szechuan peppercorns instead.

Szechuan Peppercorn Crusted Steak

Szechuan Peppercorn Spice Mix
Four 8 oz (230 g) strip loin steaks, at room
    temperature
1 Tbsp (15 mL) vegetable oil
Salt

Preheat the oven to 400°F (200°C).

Heat a cast-iron pan over high heat. Press the Szechuan peppercorn spice mix onto all sides of the steaks, ensuring that the mix adheres. Add the vegetable oil to the pan and season the steaks with salt. Once the pan is smoking hot, add the steaks and sear for 2 minutes. Turn the steaks over and transfer the pan to the oven for 5 minutes. Take the pan out of the oven and turn the steaks over and set aside. Allow the steaks to rest for 10 minutes before serving.

Sweet Potatoes

⅓ cup (80 mL) butter, melted
1 clove garlic, finely chopped
1 Tbsp (15 mL) Szechuan peppercorns,
    coarsely ground
3 Tbsp (45 mL) brown sugar
4 sweet potatoes, peeled and cut into
    ¾-inch (2 cm) rounds
1 Tbsp (15 mL) vegetable oil
Salt

Preheat the grill to medium-high heat and the oven to 400°F (200°C).

In a small pot, add the butter, garlic and Szechuan peppercorns over low heat. Cook, stirring, for 2 minutes. Add the brown sugar and cook for an additional 1 to 2 minutes, stir and remove from the heat. Toss the sweet potatoes in the vegetable oil and season them with salt. Grill the sweet potatoes on both sides, just until grill marks appear, then transfer them to a baking dish (no need to prep the dish in any way). Spoon the garlic butter mixture over the sweet potatoes. Roast the sweet potatoes for 20 to 25 minutes, until cooked through.

Creamed Spinach

1 tsp (5 mL) vegetable oil
1 shallot, diced
½ red bell pepper, diced
¾ cup (185 mL) 35% cream
1 Tbsp (15 mL) Dijon mustard
1 bunch spinach, thick stems removed
2 Tbsp (30 mL) tarragon, chopped
Juice of ½ lemon
Salt

Heat the vegetable oil in a sauté pan over high heat. Add the shallot and red pepper and sauté for 1 minute. Reduce the heat to medium. Stir together the cream and Dijon mustard and add to the vegetables. Allow this to reduce slightly, achieving a thick consistency (it should coat the back of a spoon). Add the spinach and toss until it's slightly wilted. Add the tarragon and lemon juice, mix well and season to taste with salt.

Grilled Green Onions

2 bunches green onions, roots removed
1 Tbsp (15 mL) vegetable oil
Salt
Pepper

Heat the grill to medium-high. Toss the green onions in the oil and season them with salt and pepper. Grill the green onions for 1 minute then turn them and cook for 1 minute more until they have softened and are slightly charred.

Serve all parts of this meal family-style on separate platters so that everyone can pick what they like and go back for seconds easily.

My father grew up with chickens in the yard as did his father. My grandfather always had chickens in the yard. In fact, he built a chicken coop under the house and collected the eggs. All the kids (my aunts and uncles) tended the chicken coop, collected the eggs and plucked the chickens. My grandmother taught me the proper way to blanch and pluck a chicken, a skill I don't have to call on very often these days, but one that I'm grateful to have learned from her.

Chicken is also the first meat I learned how to cut. When I was about eight years old, I stood at the kitchen counter with my dad as he showed me the different parts of the bird and where the joints were, to separate the different cuts. We used to have this old round wooden cutting board with a chip in it and an old cleaver with a dent in it, and that was the chicken cutting board. When I heard that board come out from under the sink and hit the counter I knew it was butchery time.

I wanted to show the versatility of chicken, beyond roast chicken and chicken soup, so I've included my favourite everyday chicken recipes.

Chicken is like the tofu of the meat world when you consider the way it absorbs spices and flavours. A lot of people who don't eat red meat eat a whole lot of chicken, so here are some great recipes showing the simplicity and the versatility of our ever-giving chicken.

CHICKEN

OBEDIENT INGREDIENT

Thai Basil

THAI BASIL CHICKEN SOUP *served with* ASPARAGUS *&* MUSHROOM-FILLED CRÊPES

Serves 4

The soup uses a whole chicken infused with **Thai basil**. Thai basil has a familiar but distinct flavour—similar to Western basil varieties, but with a bright, citrusy freshness. Its clean, vibrant flavour perfectly complements the subtle flavour of the chicken. If you're feeling at all under the weather this is a nice broth that will always make you feel better.

The **asparagus and mushroom-filled crêpes** are a tasty way to get vegetables into this meal. A good tip for making the crêpes is to keep the cooking temperature low. Keep it at a very moderate, even temperature. Be gentle with the crêpe, and use a good, thin-bladed spatula. Let the crêpes cool properly before you roll them—do this just before serving if possible. This recipe uses a double crêpe because they're stuffed so full.

This crêpe isn't really a starch since it's made without flour. It's really just a thin egg pancake that serves as a vehicle for the vegetable roll. Cook it, roll it with the asparagus and mushrooms and cut it with a big sharp knife so it almost looks like sushi.

Thai Basil Chicken Broth

One 2½–3 lb (1.25–1.5 kg) whole chicken
1 stalk celery, cut in half
1 medium carrot, peeled and cut in half
1 medium onion, skin removed and cut
    in half
¾ lb (375 g) shiitake mushrooms (remove
    caps and reserve for crêpes)
1 bunch Thai basil stems and leaves
1 stalk lemongrass, bruised
2 bay leaves
1 Tbsp (15 mL) ginger, smashed
1 red Thai chili, split (seeded if no heat
    is desired)
1 Tbsp (15 mL) black peppercorns
Peel of 1 lime
2–2½ quarts (1.89–2.36 L) cold water

Place all the ingredients in a large pot and cover with the water. Bring the water to a boil, then reduce the heat to a simmer, leaving the pot uncovered. Skim the top of the liquid, removing any impurities throughout the cooking process. Continue cooking for 1 hour at a low simmer.

Remove the chicken from the pot. Remove the leg meat and pull it into pieces and reserve for the soup. Remove the remaining chicken meat and reserve it for another time.

Strain the stock through a double layer of cheesecloth into a clean pot.

Store in an airtight container refrigerated for up to three days or freeze for up to one month.

Thai Basil Soup

Thai Basil Chicken Broth
¼ cup (60 mL) fish sauce
1½ Tbsp (22.5 mL) sugar
Red finger chili with seeds (optional)
Salt
Juice of 2 limes
1 cup (250 mL) leg meat (from Thai Basil
    Chicken Broth)

4 plum tomatoes, quartered, seeded and
    cut into ½-inch (1 cm) triangles
½ cucumber, peeled, seeded and sliced
1 bunch green onions, chopped
1 tsp (5 mL) sesame oil
1 lime, cut into quarters
Thai basil stem and leaves

Bring the chicken broth to a boil. Add the fish sauce, sugar, chili (if using) and lime juice. Season the soup with salt. Add the pulled chicken leg meat, the tomatoes and cucumber.

Serve the Thai basil chicken soup piping hot. Garnish each bowl with green onion, sesame oil, lime quarter and Thai basil.

Egg Crêpes

¼ cup (60 mL) melted butter
6 eggs
⅓ cup (80 mL) 2% milk
1 Tbsp (15 mL) ginger, finely minced
1 tsp (5 mL) sesame oil
1 tsp (5 mL) salt

Place 2 Tbsp (30 mL) of the melted butter in a bowl. Add the eggs, milk, ginger, sesame oil and salt and whisk well.

Heat a non-stick sauté pan over medium heat. Dab a paper towel in the remaining melted butter and coat the pan. Ladle a thin layer of the crêpe batter in the pan, coating the bottom evenly. Once the batter begins to bubble in the middle, flip the crêpe and cook for 3 to 5 seconds on the other side. Remove the crêpe from the pan and lay it on a dry kitchen towel. Repeat this process with the remaining crêpe batter. Keep the freshly cooked crêpes warm by covering them with a double layer of clean dish towels.

Assembly

3 Tbsp (45 mL) vegetable oil
Reserved shiitake mushroom caps,
    julienned (from Thai Basil Chicken
    Broth recipe)
Salt
Pepper
1 bunch asparagus (thick ends removed),
    blanched in salted water, refreshed in
    an ice bath and drained

Heat the vegetable oil in a sauté pan over medium heat. Sauté the shiitake mushroom caps over medium heat until tender, approximately 5 minutes. Season the mushroom caps with salt and pepper and set aside.

Place one crêpe on a cutting board. Place two blanched spears of asparagus lengthwise on one end of the crêpe. Place a single layer of the shiitake mushrooms over the asparagus. Roll the crêpe and place it seam side down on top of a second crêpe on the cutting board. Roll the second crêpe to enclose the first one. Cut the finished rolled crêpe on a diagonal into three pieces.

The egg crêpes are meant to be served as a side dish to complement the soup.

" This is a take on soup and a sandwich. It makes the most of everything the chicken has to offer and puts a new slant on the age-old question, "Which came first—the chicken or the egg?" (They both come at the same time in this recipe.)

ROAST CHICKEN *with* CELERIAC

Serves 4

OBEDIENT INGREDIENT Celeriac

Roasting poultry with root vegetables is very common. Simply place carrots, potatoes and parsnips around a chicken and you have a complete meal. **Celeriac** in particular goes very well with chicken: its natural sweetness brings the flavours together. As the chicken roasts on top of the celeriac and other vegetables their flavours blend, sort of like long-time lovers. Which they are.

Stuffing adds flavour. This recipe uses lemons, herbs and onions, but you can just as easily bump it up with cinnamon, limes, grapefruits; play with it. As the moisture from the lemon evaporates it creates a flavour-infusing steam that cooks the bird from the inside out.

For more about celeriac as an Obedient Ingredient, see Celeriac Soup & Gorgonzola Garlic Bread (page 113).

3 carrots, roughly diced

1 celeriac, peeled and roughly diced

1 leek, green top removed, split in half and rinsed

3 Tbsp (45 mL) vegetable oil

Salt

Pepper

1 whole chicken (about 4 lb/1.8 kg)

1 lemon, cut in half

2 shallots, roughly diced

½ bunch thyme

½ bunch sage

3–4 garlic cloves, smashed

Preheat the oven to 400°F (200°C).

Place the carrots, celeriac and leek in a large roasting pan, drizzle them with vegetable oil and season with salt and pepper. Toss the vegetables well and spread them evenly over the pan.

Season the inside of the chicken with salt and pepper. Stuff the chicken, beginning with half of the lemon, then add the shallots, thyme, sage and garlic, one after the other, ending with the other half of the lemon.

Tuck the wings under the chicken and truss the legs. Season the outside of the chicken well with salt and pepper and place it on top of the oiled vegetables.

Place the pan in the oven and roast until cooked through and the juices run clear, or until a meat thermometer reaches 185°F (85°C), approximately 2 hours.

OBEDIENT INGREDIENT

Lime Leaf

LIME LEAF CHICKEN SALAD & LIME MAYO *served with* CRUNCHY LIME TOPPING *on* CHARRED TOMATO & BROWN RICE PILAF-STYLE

Serves 4

This recipe infuses the taste of the **lime leaf** in two ways. First, it's used in the chicken broth to infuse the **chicken** with its flavour, and then it's used for a creamy mayo to keep building on this simple flavour.

The **lime mayo** is simple. Using your upright blender you can make it right in a deep measuring jug. If you can make this mayo you can make any mayo. You can add truffles or truffle oil for truffle mayo, or chilies, or any other fresh herbs or spice to flavour your mayo.

The **crunchy lime topping** is a type of fresh salsa or uncooked relish. In the same way you might put a relish or a salsa on a sandwich, I use the lime topping as a dressing. The lime and the celery supports all the existing flavours and

is another way to add fresh produce and crunch to a meal.

The **charred tomato** is a simple, warm tomato preparation. As always, buy the best tomatoes you can find and afford—plum tomatoes are at bottom of my list when I make this. It's best to make this during tomato season.

The **brown rice pilaf-style** is a basic rice recipe, but remember that brown rice soaks up a little more liquid than white. Pilaf-style means we cook the rice in the oil, sautéed with onions or any other aromatic. Each grain of rice gets coated with oil, and so absorbs the liquid individually. This creates a rice dish that has more individual and separate grains. High in fibre, full of flavour and a nice healthy option.

continued

This is a family-style meal, with the rice on the middle of the platter and servings of chicken salad on the side with roasted tomato. With a big spoon, you can serve yourself rice, chicken and vegetables in one scoop. This serving style promotes the chicken salad from a much-loved sandwich filling to sit-down dinner star. It also works with tuna or turkey salad.

Lime Mayo

1 egg yolk

1 cup (250 mL) vegetable oil

1–2 tsp (5–10 mL) Dijon mustard

Juice of 1 lime

2 lime leaves, finely chopped

Salt

Place all the ingredients in a tall container and blend using a handheld blender until thick. Transfer the mixture to a bowl and season with salt. Cover the bowl and place it in the fridge.

Store in a clean, airtight container in the fridge for up to one week. Makes 6 servings.

Lime Leaf Chicken Salad

One 3–4 lb (1.8 kg) whole chicken

3 stalks celery

2 onions, roughly chopped

2 bay leaves

1 tsp (5 mL) black peppercorns

5 lime leaves, broken

10 cups (2.5 L) cold water

Lime Mayo to taste

Salt

Place all the ingredients, except the lime mayo and salt, in a large pot and bring to a boil. Once the water comes to a boil, lower the heat to a simmer and skim the impurities that rise to the surface using a ladle. Cook, uncovered, for approximately 1 hour, then turn the heat off and allow the chicken to rest for 30 minutes. Remove the chicken from the broth and remove the skin.

Strain the broth and reserve 3¾ cups (935 mL) chicken stock for the brown rice recipe. You can then refrigerate or freeze the remaining chicken stock.

Once the chicken has cooled, shred the chicken meat by hand and place it in a bowl.

Mix the lime mayo to taste with the shredded chicken meat, season with salt and place it in the fridge until assembly.

Crunchy Lime Topping

1 cup (250 mL) celery hearts
    (approximately 6 stalks)

3 green onions, bottom whites minced,
    green tops cut into thin rings

Zest and juice of 1 lime

3 Tbsp (45 mL) olive oil

Salt to taste

Finely diced celery leaves from hearts,
    roughly torn by hand

Place all the ingredients except the celery leaves in a small bowl and mix them together.

Reserve this crunchy lime topping for assembly. Reserve the celery leaves for the final garnish.

Serve immediately. Makes 6 servings.

Charred Tomato

2 Tbsp (30 mL) olive oil

2 large tomatoes, quartered

1 tsp (5 mL) sugar

Salt

Pepper

In a cast-iron pan, heat the oil over medium to high heat. Season the tomatoes with the sugar, salt and pepper. Sear the tomatoes on both flat sides until charred then remove them from the heat and reserve until assembly.

Serve immediately.

Brown Rice Pilaf-Style

1 Tbsp (15 mL) vegetable oil

1 shallot, finely diced

1½ cups (375 mL) brown rice

1 bay leaf

3¾ (935 mL) cups chicken stock from chicken salad recipe

1 Tbsp (15 mL) soy sauce

Heat the vegetable oil in a large, rimmed pot over medium heat. Add the shallot and cook until tender and translucent. Add the rice and bay leaf and stir to coat the rice in the oil. Add the chicken stock and the soy sauce and stir again. Bring to a boil, reduce to a low simmer and place the lid ajar over the pot. Cook until the rice is tender, approximately 30 to 40 minutes, and remove from heat. Fluff with a fork and set aside, covered to keep warm.

"This meal is an easy midweek meal, a great way to feed groups of people and a great weekend treat. You can find lime leaves in most Asian grocery stores, fresh or frozen, and the frozen works almost as well as the fresh. Both are packed with flavour.

Assembly

Brown Rice Pilaf-Style

Charred Tomatoes

Lime Leaf Chicken Salad

Crunchy Lime Topping

Celery leaves

4 tsp (20 mL) olive oil

Place brown rice on each serving plate. Place two pieces of charred tomato overtop, followed by equal amounts of the lime leaf chicken salad on top of the charred tomato. Spoon the crunchy lime topping overtop the salad.

Garnish each plate with some celery leaves and a drizzle of olive oil.

This is perfect with Sparkling Limeade (page 174).

Peanuts

MALAYSIAN-INSPIRED CHICKEN WINGS

Serves 4

Instead of by deep-frying we get the crunch on these wings by roasting. The sugar caramelizes, producing wings that are juicy with a little bit of crunch.

The longer you marinate the better. These wings can marinate for two days, which will make the meat flavourful right to the bone. Score the flesh of the wings so the marinade can penetrate the meat. The **peanut butter marinade** is also great on beef or pork.

We tend to see fried wings served with fried potatoes and carrots and dip, but I like to serve these with **rice noodles**. I boil the noodles quickly, sprinkle them with carrots and roasted peanuts, then drizzle them with warm vinaigrette. The wings become a meal with this noodle salad.

Peanuts are a noteworthy allergen (to the point that they've been banned from many schools), but if you are not allergic to them, this dish is a tasty opportunity to use them.

A chicken wing is really the perfect vehicle for a sauce and this recipe is a good introduction to making a peanut sauce. Peanut sauce on a satay has almost become a mainstream classic, so we're substituting the spicy barbecue chicken wing sauce with a variation of a peanut satay sauce.

Peanut Butter Marinade

2 cups (500 mL) smooth natural
    peanut butter
8 cloves garlic, minced
1 cup (250 mL) soy sauce
½ cup (125 mL) brown sugar
½ cup (125 mL) water
Juice of 2 limes
Zest of 1 lime
1 tsp (5 mL) cayenne
½ tsp (2.5 mL) freshly ground black
    pepper

Place all the ingredients into a large bowl, stir to incorporate and set aside.

Store in a clean, airtight container in the fridge for up to three days. Makes enough for 4 portions of wings.

Peanut Butter Chicken Wings

24 chicken wings
Peanut Butter Marinade

Score the chicken wings to allow the marinade to penetrate the meat. Place the chicken wings in the peanut butter marinade. In a stainless steel bowl, and using your hands, massage the wings into the peanut butter marinade, cover the bowl with plastic wrap and then place the wings in the fridge for 30 minutes to a maximum of 24 hours.

Preheat the oven to 350°F (175°C). Line a large baking tray with parchment paper. Place the peanut butter chicken wings on the tray and bake them in the oven until the meat is cooked and the wings are crisp and golden brown, 30 to 45 minutes. Halfway through the cooking time turn the wings over to brown both sides.

Peanut Crunch

Peanut oil for frying
2 red finger chillies, cut in half, seeded
    and sliced
5 Tbsp (75 mL) cornstarch
Salt
2 shallots, peeled cut in half and sliced
1 cup (250 mL) toasted peanuts, finely
    chopped

Fill a large pot one-third full of peanut oil and heat to 350°F (175°C). Line a baking tray with paper towels. Place the chilies in a bowl, coat well with 2 Tbsp (30 mL) of the cornstarch and fry them until golden brown. Remove the chilies from the oil and place them on the lined baking tray. Season the chilies with salt and set them aside.

Place the shallots in the same bowl, coat well with the remaining 3 Tbsp

(45 mL) of cornstarch and fry until golden brown. Remove the shallots from the oil and place them on another baking tray lined with paper towels. Season the shallots with salt and set aside.

Place the crispy fried chilies and shallots on a cutting board and chop finely. Combine the chopped peanuts with the fried chilies and shallots in a bowl and set aside.

Store in a paper-lined, airtight container at room temperature for up to two days. Makes 4 portions

Rice Wine Vinegar Dressing

1 cup (250 mL) seasoned rice wine vinegar
1 clove garlic, minced
Zest of 1 lime
1 tsp (5 mL) sesame oil
Salt to taste

Place all the ingredients in a bowl, stir and set aside.

Store in a clean, airtight container in the fridge for up to three days. Makes 4 portions.

Rice Noodle Salad

One 8 oz (227 g) package vermicelli rice noodles, cooked according to package directions
Rice Wine Vinegar Dressing
Peanut Crunch
2 cups (500 mL) bean sprouts
1 carrot, peeled and julienned
1 English cucumber, peeled, seeded and diced
½ bunch green onions, sliced thinly on the bias
½ bunch cilantro leaves, leaves picked

Place the cooked rice noodles in the centre of a serving plate and dress with half of the rice wine vinegar dressing. Scatter the peanut crunch over the rice noodles. Place the bean sprouts over the rice noodles. Place the carrots around the outside of the rice noodles and bean sprouts. Scatter the cucumber and green onion over the carrots. Then pour the remaining rice wine vinegar dressing overtop the rice noodle salad.

Place the peanut butter chicken wings on the rice noodle salad and garnish with the picked cilantro.

OBEDIENT INGREDIENT

Blood Orange

CRISPY CHICKEN FINGERS *served with* SWEET & SOUR BLOOD ORANGE SAUCE & BLOOD ORANGE WATERCRESS SALAD

Serves 4

Instead of just putting salt and pepper on a chicken, add more flavour by using all of a blood orange: use the zests to make the rub, with fennel and black peppercorns, then do a flour, egg and panko as you would for making a basic fried cutlet.

Breading chicken can be easier if you just use forks—one for the chicken, another for the egg and another for the panko—your hands stay clean and so does your countertop.

Kids love the familiarity of the **crispy chicken fingers** but when they bite into them they get a different flavour, making this a great way to introduce them to new flavours.

I make about 50 chicken fingers on a Sunday, cook them all and put them in the freezer on a flat sheet to freeze.

Then I bag them up and when I need something quick on a weeknight I thaw them and reheat them for dinner. I make the sauce in batches during the week and thaw it as I need it as well. You can also cut these chicken strips into bite-size pieces to make nuggets.

Many sweet and sour sauces start as an infused citrus sauce. The **blood orange dipping sauce**, which has a lovely vibrant colour, has a few ingredients that round out the tart of the citrus. The cornstarch gives the sauce a familiar consistency.

I figure the chicken fingers take up enough prep time, so I've made the **blood orange watercress salad** recipe super-quick and easy.

Blood Orange Rub

Zest of 1 blood orange, chopped
1 Tbsp (15 mL) garlic powder
2 tsp (10 mL) fennel seed, ground in a
     mortar and pestle
½ Tbsp (7.5 mL) black pepper
1 tsp (5 mL) vegetable oil

Combine all the ingredients in a clean,
dry bowl and set aside until you are ready
to assemble the chicken fingers.

Use immediately. Makes 4 portions.

Crispy Chicken Fingers

4 boneless, skinless chicken breasts
     (6 oz/175 g each), cut into strips
Blood Orange Rub
Vegetable oil for frying
1 cup (250 mL) all-purpose flour, seasoned
     with salt and pepper
2 eggs, whisked
2½ cups (625 mL) panko breadcrumbs
Salt
Pepper

Coat the chicken strips with the blood
orange rub and place them in the fridge
for 30 minutes.

Preheat the oven to 350°F (175°C).

Fill a large pot one-third full of vegetable oil and heat it to 350°F (175°C). Place
three dishes side by side on the counter.
Place flour in one, whisked eggs in
another and panko in the last dish.

Remove chicken from the fridge and
season it with salt and pepper. Dredge the
chicken strips on both sides in the flour,
followed by the eggs and then the panko
breadcrumbs. Place the breaded chicken
on a baking tray lined with a cooling rack.

In batches, place the chicken strips
in the heated oil and fry until crispy and
golden. Place the cooked chicken fingers
on a baking tray and keep warm in the
oven, approximately 5 minutes. (You can

cook them in a preheated 350°F (175°C)
oven for approximately 35 minutes, but
let's face it, they don't taste as good! Heh
heh!) Repeat this process with the remaining chicken fingers.

Enjoy with the Sweet and Sour Blood
Orange Sauce on the side. No double-
dipping!

Sweet and Sour Blood Orange Sauce

1 Tbsp (15 mL) olive oil
½ red onion, diced
1 cup (250 mL) honey
½ cup (125 mL) red wine vinegar
½ cup (125 mL) water
4 blood oranges, peeled and roughly
     chopped
Zest of 2 blood oranges
1 cinnamon stick
Salt
Pepper
1 Tbsp (15 mL) cornstarch mixed with
     2 Tbsp (30 mL) cold water
8 basil leaves, julienned

Heat the olive oil in a sauté pan over
medium heat. Add the red onion and
sweat until tender and translucent. Mix
the honey, red wine vinegar and ½ cup
(125 mL) water in a bowl, add to the sauté
pan and stir. Add the blood oranges, zest
and cinnamon stick, and stir. Season with
salt and pepper, stir and cook until the
mixture has reduced by half.

Strain the mixture through a sieve
into a clean pot over medium heat. Add
the cornstarch and cold water mix to the
blood orange sauce and stir. Bring the
blood orange mixture to a simmer and
continue to cook for approximately 3 to
5 minutes. Remove from the heat and stir
in the basil.

Store in an airtight container in the
fridge for up to 24 hours. After that, the corn-

starch will lose its holding power. Makes
4 portions.

Blood Orange Watercress Salad

2 blood oranges
3 Tbsp (45 mL) olive oil
1 Tbsp (15 mL) red wine vinegar
1 shallot, diced
Salt
Pepper
2 cups (500 mL) iceberg lettuce, roughly
     chopped
1 bunch watercress, trimmed
½ cup (125 mL) crushed rice crackers

Segment the blood oranges over a sieve
and bowl to save all the juice and set the
segments aside. Place the olive oil, red
wine vinegar and shallot in the blood
orange juice, season with salt and pepper
and stir.

Place the iceberg lettuce and watercress on a serving plate. Spoon the blood
orange dressing over the greens.

Garnish with blood orange segments
and crushed rice crackers.

> " I made these for my
> daughter's birthday party
> one year. The blood orange
> is a take on the classic sweet
> and sour or plum sauce.

OBEDIENT INGREDIENT

Coconut

COCONUT BAKED CHICKEN *served with* MIN DIPPING SAUCE

Serves 4

I really like the sweet and savoury mix, the texture of the **coconut** and that feeling of something crunchy without deep frying that comes in this chicken dish. The cooking times may vary depending on the size of the chicken pieces.

If you cut up a whole chicken try to keep the size of the cuts uniform, but if that's impossible, just keep an eye on them while they're cooking.

I like to add a flavourful moist sauce whenever I do chicken that has a crust so it doesn't get too dry. This **mint dipping sauce** is an herb paste that adds a nice refreshing complement to the chicken. The mint cuts right through the soft richness of the coconut.

Shredded, dried, fresh, jellied—these are some of the ways you can enjoy coconut. Surely one of these ways (or just the water of the coconut) will appeal to the pickiest of eaters. I take advantage of coconut in other recipes as well; see Papaya Barbecue Chicken & Spiced Cashew Nuts served with Coconut Rice & Watercress Papaya Salad (page 75), Pasta Salad with Green Onion Dressing (page 108) and Pistachio Macaroons (page 171).

> "This is a baked take on the idea of Southern fried chicken inspired by coconut shrimp.

Mint Dipping Sauce

1 cup (250 mL) coconut milk
1 large bunch of mint, leaves picked
Zest and juice of 1 lime
1 tsp (5 mL) sugar
Salt

Place all the ingredients in a blender and purée until smooth. Transfer the mint dipping sauce to a bowl and place it in the refrigerator until needed.

Store in a clean, airtight container in the fridge for up to two days. Makes 4 portions.

Coconut Baked Chicken

1 whole chicken, cut into pieces to match the size of the chicken thigh
2 Tbsp (30 mL) vegetable oil
2 tsp (10 mL) garlic powder
¼ tsp (1 mL) cayenne (optional)
¾ cup (185 mL) shredded unsweetened coconut
½ cup (125 mL) panko (or coarse breadcrumbs)
Salt
Pepper

Preheat the oven to 375°F (190°C) and line a baking tray with parchment paper.

Place the chicken in a bowl, drizzle with the vegetable oil and toss to coat. Season with the garlic powder and cayenne and toss again to coat the spices.

Place the shredded coconut and panko in a resealable bag. In batches, place the chicken pieces inside the bag, close it and shake it to distribute the coconut and panko evenly. Remove the chicken pieces from the bag and place them on the lined baking tray.

Repeat this process with the remaining chicken.

Place the tray in the oven and bake until the chicken pieces are golden brown and cooked through, approximately 45 minutes.

In North America we tend to lean on salmon—a lot. Now, I love salmon, and I have included a good salmon recipe here, but there's more to midweek fish than salmon.

Not only that, we've overfished and now have a seafood crisis. If we're not mindful of this crisis we'll lose many species. Seachoice, a group of five Canadian conservation organizations, maintains a database of sustainable seafood choices (http://www.seachoice.org).

I like my fish as fresh as possible. In Trinidad I'll go to the market (some of the markets are right at the dock) and wait until the fish is unloaded off the boats. Fresh fish should be odourless with bright gills and bulging, clear eyes. If you see fish on sale without its gills, stay away from it because the vendors are trying to hide the fact that the fish isn't fresh. Get your fishmonger to scale the fish for you to save the mess at home—they're prepared for it. They can also fillet your whole fish. Get to know your fishmonger, throw them an extra couple of bucks and remember them during the holidays. They'll take care of you for life.

These recipes show that fish can be a fast and flexible midweek meal. We bread it and fry it up in a pan, we grill it, we wrap it in an easy little packet.

Diets follow trends and sometimes we encounter diets that say to eat only fish. In the words of my grandmother, I say "All things in moderation."

FISH

Salt Cod

SALT COD FRITTERS *with* CREAMY MUSTARD SAUCE *&* ORANGE CHILI SAUCE *&* PINEAPPLE CHUTNEY *served with* SHREDDED ZUCCHINI SALAD

Serves 4

We make akra in the Caribbean, but if I said "akra" you might say "ak-what??" It's easier to call akra "fritters." And I love these fritters—they're like a savoury fish donut.

The sauce is a take on a tartar sauce. So the classic fried fish and tartar sauce becomes **salt cod akra** and **creamy mustard sauce**.

What I love about the **orange chili sauce** is that it's a no-cook chili sauce. Canning a chili sauce can be a real ordeal as you try to get the right mix of acid and vinegar for preserving, so this is a no-cook method. It won't last as long in your fridge but it's so easy you can make it every day. You throw a whole orange minus its skin into the blender, toss in the rest of the ingredients and whoosh—a perfect blend of flavour with just the right consistency.

You can find dried salt cod at Portuguese, Spanish and Caribbean grocery stores, or rehydrated and frozen salt cod in Chinese grocery stores. You can't eat salt cod in its dried state. You need to soak it for about 24 hours in water, changing the water three times to draw out the salt and rehydrate the fish. The salting process was introduced

continued

so that fish wouldn't spoil before it got to market.

In the Caribbean we sauté salt cod with tomatoes and eat it for breakfast with a fried or roasted bread called *bake*. The French make it into a paste to be enjoyed with bread, and the Spanish add it to stews. I like all these uses, but I especially love to make akra.

To cook a fritter, simply take a tablespoon of the fritter mix and let it drop carefully into hot oil. Too big and it'll be doughy inside. Too small and it'll burn. About a tablespoon-size dollop seems to work well. You want a natural rustic shape, so don't worry about making the fritters uniform but do make sure they are evenly sized. Keep the oil at a moderate temperature, around 350°F (175°C), to guarantee browning and cooking through.

These fritters make an excellent meal, but they're also a fantastic snack food for a party or as part of a bigger spread. They're best eaten fresh with one of the delicious dipping sauces I've included.

The **shredded zucchini salad** recipe is based on a coleslaw technique and has a very clean flavour. After grating the zucchini you cure it by adding salt to draw out the moisture, then rinse it and squeeze out the excess salt. The zucchini becomes soft and tender, and the essence of the salt seasons the salad. It's a different approach to zucchini.

The **pineapple chutney** is a version of one of my restaurant recipes. I would serve chutney with poppadums instead of bread when guests were seated, to prepare them for what was to come. It is one of my favourite recipe-creation memories and the dish served to set the mood of the evening well.

Salt Cod Fritters

Vegetable oil for frying

1 lb (500 g) salt cod, soaked in ample water to cover the fish completely for 24 hours, changing water 3 times until cod no longer tastes of salt

3 cups all-purpose flour

2 Tbsp (30 mL) baking powder

2 tsp (10 mL) baking soda

1 tsp (5 mL) salt

3 cups (750 mL) 2% milk

3 eggs

1 cup (250 mL) cilantro stems and leaves, finely chopped

Half-fill a deep pot with the oil and heat it to 350°F (175°C) (use a thermometer for accuracy). Line a baking tray with three layers of paper towel.

Remove the salt cod from the water, pat it dry and roughly chop. Place it in a food processor and pulse until shredded. Remove the salt cod, squeeze it with your hands to remove any excess water and place it in a clean, dry bowl.

Place the dry ingredients in a large bowl and mix. In a separate bowl, whisk the milk and eggs and add them to the

dry ingredients. Add the salt cod and cilantro, and fold to incorporate. Spoon 1 Tbsp (15 mL) of salt cod batter into the hot oil, ensuring you do not crowd the oil with too many fritters at one time. Fry until golden brown and cooked through, approximately 3 minutes, turning the fritters over once while cooking. Remove the salt cod fritters from the hot oil, place them on the lined baking tray and season to taste with salt and pepper.

Serve the fritters while still hot, preferably along with the assorted sauces (see facing page) for a variety of flavour experiences with each new fritter. The zucchini salad (see facing page) can be served on the side along with the dish, in the same way as fish and chips are often served with coleslaw.

Creamy Mustard Sauce

1 cup (250 mL) sour cream (reduced fat
   if you prefer)
4 sweet gherkins, minced
2 Tbsp (30 mL) yellow mustard
1 Tbsp (15 mL) ground coriander seed
   (use a mortar and pestle)
1 tsp (5 mL) honey
Salt to taste

Place all the ingredients into a bowl, mix,
cover and place in the fridge until serving
time. Enjoy with salt cod fritters.

*Store in an airtight container refrigerated
for up to one week.*

Orange Chili Sauce

1 large orange, peeled and roughly
   chopped
¼ red onion, roughly chopped
1 red finger chili, with seeds, roughly
   chopped
1 green finger chili, with seeds, roughly
   chopped
2 tsp (10 mL) sugar
2 tsp (10 mL) salt
1½ tsp (2.5 mL) white wine vinegar

Place all the ingredients in a blender and
purée until smooth. Transfer to a bowl
and enjoy with salt cod fritters.

*Store refrigerated in an airtight container
for up to two days.*

Pineapple Chutney

1 Tbsp (15 mL) vegetable oil
½ red onion, finely diced
1 pineapple, peeled and cut into a large
   dice
½ cup (125 mL) sugar
¼ cup (60 mL) white wine vinegar
1 tsp (5 mL) fennel seed
Salt

Heat the oil in a sauté pan over medium
heat. Add the red onion and sauté until
tender and translucent. Add the pineapple,
sugar, vinegar and fennel seed. Stir well.
Once the pineapple has softened slightly
and the juices have reduced, approximately 7 to 10 minutes, remove from the
heat. Allow to cool to room temperature
then season to taste. Serve at room temperature.

*Store refrigerated in an airtight container
for up to four days.*

Shredded Zucchini Salad

¼ red onion, julienned
Juice of 2 limes
1 tsp (5 mL) salt
1 large zucchini, grated
1 cup (250 mL) cherry tomato halves
¼ cup (60 mL) cilantro, roughly chopped

Place the red onion, lime juice and salt in
a small bowl. Stir, then set aside.

Place the grated zucchini in a large bowl
and sprinkle with salt. Allow to sit for
5 minutes. Transfer to a strainer and rinse
well with cold water. Allow to drain fully
or squeeze out excess moisture with your
hands. Transfer to a clean, dry, serving
bowl.

Add the remaining ingredients and the
onion mixture to the zucchini, toss to
incorporate, and serve.

Saffron

SAFFRON HALIBUT PACKETS *served with* SAFFRON RICE *&* SAUTÉED PEPPERS

Serves 4

There is a technique in French cooking called *en pau-piette*, which means to cook in a package. Traditionally the package is parchment paper, and the food steams inside it. When the package is brought to the table and cut open you get this incredible aroma, that serves as a teaser for the meal you are about to enjoy.

It is important to rehydrate **saffron** in a bit of liquid before you use it. One way of doing this is to make what's known as **saffron tea**. The saffron tints the wine (and con-sequently the entire dish) a little bit ; the wine adds flavour to the whole dish. Wine and fish are a natural complement to each other.

In this recipe, the **halibut packets** are served on top of the **peppers**, which are served on top of the **saffron rice,** to make a complete meal. You can make the packets ahead of time, before you go to work. Then when you come home, you can start the rice, put the packet in the oven, sauté your peppers and look like a champion.

Saffron Tea

2 tsp (10 mL) saffron
1 Tbsp (15 mL) dry white wine

Add the saffron to the white wine and steep for 10 minutes. Leave the saffron in the wine.

Saffron Halibut Packets

Four 6 oz (175 g) skinless halibut fillets
Saffron Tea
2 carrots, thinly sliced on a bias
1½ Tbsp (22.5 mL) capers, drained and rinsed
¼ cup (60 mL) white wine
Zest and juice of 1 orange
1 Tbsp (15 mL) butter
Salt
1 bunch green onions, top third sliced for garnish, mid third kept whole, bottom whites reserved for rice
Pepper

Place the fillets on a plate, stain each one with a few threads of saffron from the saffron tea, making sure to leave in some of the threads, then refrigerate for 15 to 20 minutes.

Preheat the oven to 400°F (200°C).

In a sauté pan, add the saffron tea with the carrots, capers, white wine and orange zest and juice. Bring up to a simmer and cook until the carrots are slightly tender, approximately 2 minutes. Add the butter, season with salt, stir and remove from the heat.

Prepare four pieces of parchment paper or foil large enough to wrap the fish in. Place the whole green onion pieces in the centre of the parchment paper or foil. Layer the carrot mixture over the whole green onion pieces. Season the halibut with salt and pepper, then place it over the carrot mixture. Spoon the sauce from the vegetables over the fish, then fold in

the edges, creating a sealed packet.

Place the packets on a baking tray with the seams of the package down and bake in the oven until the fish is cooked through, approximately 10 minutes. Once cooked, open the packets and garnish with the green onion slices.

Saffron Rice

1 Tbsp (15 mL) butter
Reserved green onion whites, smashed and roughly chopped
1 clove garlic, chopped
1 tsp (5 mL) dried saffron
2 cups (500 mL) parboiled long-grain white rice
4 cups (1 L) cold water
Salt

In a pot, melt the butter over medium heat; add the reserved green onion whites and garlic, and sweat until tender. Add the saffron and stir. Add the rice and stir, ensuring the rice is coated with saffron. Add the water and stir. Bring to a boil, cover and reduce the heat to a simmer. Cook for 25 minutes until the rice is cooked. Season with salt.

Sautéed Peppers

2 Tbsp (30 mL) olive oil
1 clove garlic, chopped
1 green chili, sliced, seeds removed
1 red bell pepper, julienned
1 orange bell pepper, julienned
1 yellow bell pepper, julienned
¼ red onion, sliced

"Saffron is one of the most expensive ingredients on the planet, but it is used sparingly due to its strong flavour. It is hand-harvested from the saffron crocus flower, which yields three stigmas that are dried and sold as saffron. It has an aromatic, very distinct floral flavour and is popular in sauces and soups, and with rice. You either love it or you don't. And if you've never tried it, it's well worth experimenting with. Store it in a cool dry dark place to preserve its aroma and colour.

Zest and juice of 1 lemon
Salt

In a sauté pan, add 1 Tbsp (15 mL) of the olive oil and sweat the garlic and green chili over medium heat. Add the peppers and sauté for 1 minute. Add the red onion and lemon zest and sauté until slightly tender. Remove from the heat, season with salt and drizzle with the lemon juice and remaining 1 Tbsp (15 mL) of olive oil.

Place the rice on the centre of the plate. Remove the halibut and all of its contents and place on top of the rice. Place sautéed peppers all around the plate and serve all hot.

OBEDIENT INGREDIENT

Edamame

SHORELINE FRIED HALIBUT *served with* TOFU FRIES & SOY SAUCE AIOLI & MUSHY EDAMAME

Serves 4

A spiced **soy milk marinade** keeps the fish juicy; the garlic, onion and pepper in the marinade supply a bit of bite.

The **tofu fries** are crispy and crunchy on the outside but soft and delicious on the inside.

What I love about this menu is the way the obedient ingredient, **edamame**, works as an entry point to draw us into the world of soy. Soy milk is in the marinade, soy tofu is used for the fries and edamame are the mushy peas. This one simple ingredient opens a gateway from a very familiar dish, fish and chips, and leads us to an unexpected destination.

Spiced Soy Milk Marinade

1 cup (250 mL) soy milk

1 Tbsp (15 mL) garlic powder

1 Tbsp (15 mL) onion powder

1 tsp (5 mL) black pepper

½ tsp (2.5 mL) cayenne

Pour the soy milk in a wide baking dish. Whisk in the garlic powder, onion powder, black pepper and cayenne.

Shoreline Fried Halibut

1½ lb (750 g) halibut, cut into 1½ oz (45 g) pieces

Spiced Soy Milk Marinade

1 cup (250 mL) vegetable oil for frying

1 cup (250 mL) all-purpose flour

Salt

Pepper

Add the halibut pieces to the marinade, and refrigerate for at least 30 minutes, to a maximum of 24 hours.

In a large, heavy-bottomed or cast-iron pan, heat the vegetable oil to 350°F (175°C) over medium-high heat. Use enough oil so that the pot or pan is one-third full.

Line a baking tray with paper towel. Place the flour in a paper bag.

Remove the halibut from the marinade and place a few pieces at a time in the paper bag. Shake well to coat in flour and cook in the hot oil.

Turn halibut over on all sides until golden brown, approximately 3 to 5 min-

utes. Remove the halibut from heat and place on three layers of paper towels to absorb any excess oil and season with salt and pepper. Repeat with the remaining halibut.

Tofu Fries

Vegetable oil for frying

½ cup (125 mL) cornstarch

1¼ lb (625 g) extra-firm tofu, drained, cut into ¾-inch (2 cm) sticks

Salt

Fill a large pot to no more than one-third full with the oil and heat to 350°F (175°C). Line a baking tray with paper towel.

Place the cornstarch in a bowl. In batches, coat the tofu with cornstarch and gently place in the hot oil, separating the tofu fries as they cook to prevent sticking. Remove the tofu fries from the oil once they're golden brown, transfer to three layers of paper towels and season with salt. Repeat with the remaining tofu.

Soy Sauce Mayo

½ cup (125 mL) mayonnaise

1 Tbsp (15 mL) soy sauce

¼ tsp (1 mL) sesame oil

Place all the ingredients in a bowl, mix well, cover and place in the fridge until ready to serve.

Store in an airtight container refrigerated for up to one week.

"Edamame is soy bean, and this recipe plays with all the derivatives of soy for its take on the everyday classic of fish and chips with mushy peas. Classic fish and chips comprises halibut in a batter, deep-fried potato french fries and mushy peas with lemon or malt vinegar. This version has a shallow-fried fish, tofu fries and mushy edamame. It was inspired by my friend Justin, who catches fish up north, cuts them into fillets and shallow-fries them in a pan over a campfire.

Mushy Edamame

3 cups frozen, shelled edamame

¼ cup (60 mL) olive oil

Salt

Boil the edamame in heavily salted water until soft and tender, approximately 20 minutes. Reserve 1 cup (250 mL) of the cooking water and drain the edamame. Place the edamame, ½ cup (125 mL) of the reserved cooking liquid and the olive oil in a blender. Purée until smooth, adding more cooking water if necessary. Remove from the blender, season with salt and set aside to cool.

Serve three to five pieces of halibut per person along with healthy-sized dollops of the condiments and a wedge of lemon.

Nori

NORI-CRUSTED SALMON *served with*
SOBA NOODLE SALAD *&* GREEN TEA

Serves 4

In North America, **nori** gets introduced to most people as the dark, papery stuff that holds together a California roll. But it is so much more than a wrapper, and this dish proves that.

Because this dish lives in the world of Japanese cuisine I'm using my favourite buckwheat soba noodle as the starch for the cold or room-temp **soba noodle salad**. Boiling the noodles before covering them in a warm dressing helps the noodles to separate and embeds the flavour of the dressing. A lot of crunchy fresh ingredients are the final touch. Consider this an updated take on a pasta salad.

The **vinaigrette** continues the Japanese theme with its rice wine vinegar, soy sauce, ginger and sesame oil.

I really like **salmon**. Some foodies think it's too much of an everyday fish—and maybe it is. But it's everyday because it is not a shy fish: it has a good, full flavour (there's nothing neutral about it) and a very distinct colour. It's a coldwater fish and therefore has some fat, which keeps it juicy as it cooks and helps it maintain its own distinct flavour.

Nori Crust

2 nori sheets, toasted

1½ Tbsp (22.5 mL) sesame seeds

1 tsp (5 mL) sweet paprika

1 tsp (5 mL) black peppercorns

Salt to taste

2 Tbsp (30 mL) butter

1 shallot, minced

1 clove garlic, minced

1 Thai chili, sliced and seeds removed

In a mortar and pestle, break up the nori sheets. Add the sesame seeds, paprika, black peppercorns and salt. Grind to combine.

In a small sauté pan, melt the butter over medium heat. Add the shallot and garlic. Sauté over medium heat for 1 minute until the shallot and garlic soften and turn slightly brown. Add the chili and the nori spice mixture. Stir for 1 to 2 minutes to toast then remove from the heat.

Nori-Crusted Salmon

1 Tbsp (15 mL) butter

1 tsp (5 mL) vegetable oil

Four 5–6 oz (150–175 g) salmon fillets, skin removed

Salt

Nori Crust

Preheat the oven to 350°F (175°C).

Heat the butter and oil in a sauté pan. Season the fillets on all sides with salt. Sear the salmon skin side up. Turn and sear on the other side, approximately 2 minutes in total. Transfer the salmon fillets to a baking dish, set them skin side down and pat the nori crust overtop. Bake in the oven until cooked through, 5 to 7 minutes.

Soba Vinaigrette

½ cup (125 mL) seasoned rice wine vinegar

¼ cup (60 mL) soy sauce

1 Tbsp (15 mL) minced ginger

2 tsp (10 mL) sesame oil

¼ cup (60 mL) vegetable oil

In a bowl, add the seasoned rice wine vinegar, soy sauce, ginger and sesame oil. Slowly add the vegetable oil, whisking until completely combined.

Store in an airtight container refrigerated for up to three days.

Soba Noodle Salad

1 Tbsp (15 mL) vegetable oil

½ lb (250 g) shiitake mushroom caps, sliced

Salt

1 clove garlic, minced

1 Tbsp (15 mL) minced ginger

2 cups (500 mL) sugar snap peas, blanched and thinly sliced on a bias

1 carrot, julienned

1 bunch garlic chives (or green onion), cut into 1-inch (2.5 cm) pieces on a bias

Pepper

Soba Vinaigrette

¾ lb (375 g) soba noodles

1 nori sheet, cut into 1-inch (2.5 cm) pieces, for garnish

2 Tbsp (30 mL) sesame seeds, for garnish

In a large sauté pan, heat the vegetable oil over medium heat. Add the shiitake mushrooms, season with salt and sauté for 7 to 10 minutes. Add the garlic and ginger, and sauté for 1 minute. Add the sugar snap peas, carrot and garlic chives, and stir. Season with salt and pepper, then sauté for 2 to 3 minutes. Add 3 Tbsp (45 mL) of

" Nori is dried seaweed that we mostly know as the wrap for sushi. It's a healthy, fibrous vitamin-rich food—and great paired with salmon. In this recipe the nori is treated not as a wrap but as an ingredient to make a crust. The recipe follows a simple process of pan-searing (or grilling) then crusting and baking like never before.

the vinaigrette, combine well then remove the pan from the heat.

Boil the soba noodles, following the package directions, until cooked through. Lay the noodles on a tray and spoon the remaining vinaigrette overtop. Allow the noodles to absorb the vinaigrette for 5 minutes.

In a bowl, toss the vegetables and soba noodles together. Place the nori-crusted salmon on top of the soba noodle salad and garnish with nori pieces and sesame seeds.

Green Tea

Water, boiled

1 Tbsp (15 mL) green tea leaves

Pour hot water in a teapot and cups to warm them then pour the water out. Place the green tea in the teapot. Pour water in the pot and steep for approximately 20 seconds. Pour the water out to remove sediment from tea. Refill teapot with water. Steep for 1 minute. Pour into teacups. Enjoy.

OBEDIENT INGREDIENT

Lemongrass

LEMONGRASS BAKED SNAPPER *served with* GINGER BUTTER POTATOES & CRISPY GARLIC BROCCOLI

Serves 4

Lemongrass has taken off in popularity in tandem with the rise in Thai cooking across North America. I love lemongrass and its distinct citrus flavour, which marries well with so many ingredients.

Snapper is a tasty saltwater fish that is a natural pairing with lemongrass. In Southeast Asia they make a fish broth with lemongrass, or bake a whole fish stuffed with lemongrass, so this pairing has a history. The inspiration for this recipe is a fish stew common in both the Mediterranean and the Caribbean and often containing tomatoes. The twist here is the addition of lemongrass to tomatoes, and the use of yellow tomatoes instead of red.

Broccoli with crispy garlic is a simple yet appetizing side. Broccoli is included in this meal because it is such a North American staple.

This menu, with its lemongrass, ginger and garlic, may seem like a lot of big flavours, but each one is done in a different way. The garlic is crispy, the lemongrass is complementary and the **ginger butter log** is guaranteed to bump up your **potatoes** (see page 157). Each flavour works with the other, making this a very delicious meal.

Ginger Butter Log

1 cup (250 mL) butter
2 Tbsp (30 mL) finely minced ginger

Melt the butter in a small pot over low heat. Add the ginger and whisk to combine. Transfer to a bowl and place in the freezer. After 5 minutes, whisk again and return to the freezer for another 5 to 10 minutes, until the butter has solidified.

Place a large piece of plastic wrap on a board. Spread the ginger butter in the centre of the plastic wrap. Roll the plastic wrap over and twist the ends to create a log. Place the ginger butter in the fridge until needed.

Store refrigerated wrapped airtight in plastic for up to one week. Alternatively, store in freezer wrapped airtight in plastic for up to one month.

Yellow Tomato Sauce

3 Tbsp (45 mL) olive oil
3 cloves garlic, minced
3 lemongrass stalks, bruised (keep bottom 2 inches/5 cm and tops for snapper)
1 large shallot, finely diced
½ cup (125 mL) dry white wine
5½ cups (1.37 L) roughly chopped yellow tomatoes
Zest of 1 lemon
Salt

Heat the oil in a large, wide-based pot over medium heat. Add the garlic, lemongrass stalks and shallot. Sauté until the garlic and shallot are slightly golden. Deglaze with the white wine and reduce by two-thirds over high heat, approximately 1 to 2 minutes. Add the tomatoes, stir and cook for 15 minutes. Remove from the heat, add the lemon zest and season with salt.

Store refrigerated in airtight container for up to three days.

Lemongrass Baked Snapper

3 reserved lemongrass tops and bottom 2 inches (5 cm), finely chopped (reserved from Yellow Tomato Sauce recipe)
1 bunch green onion, white bottoms separated, green tops finely chopped
Yellow Tomato Sauce
2 Tbsp (30 mL) olive oil
Four 5–6 oz (150–175 g) snapper fillets, cut in half with 1-inch (2.5 cm) slits cut along skin
Salt
Pepper

Preheat the oven to 450°F (230°C) with the middle rack in place.

Place the lemongrass tops along the bottom of a baking dish large enough to hold all the ingredients without crowding the pan and arrange the green onion whites overtop. Spoon half of the yellow tomato sauce, including its lemongrass stalks, over the green onion whites. Oil the fillet pieces with the olive oil and season with salt and pepper. Place the fillet pieces over the tomato sauce, skin side up. Place the chopped lemongrass bottoms inside the slits in the fillet pieces. Spoon the remaining sauce over the snapper.

Bake in the oven until the snapper is cooked through, approximately 15 minutes. Garnish with the reserved chopped green onion tops.

Crispy Garlic Broccoli

2 Tbsp (30 mL) vegetable oil
3 cloves garlic, thinly sliced
1 bunch broccoli, cut into pieces and blanched
Salt

Heat the oil in a sauté pan over medium heat. Place the garlic in the pan and fry until crispy, tossing constantly, approximately 5 minutes. Add the broccoli, toss to incorporate and then remove from the heat. Season with salt and serve alongside the snapper.

For a complete meal, serve with Ginger Butter Potatoes (see page 157).

Even people who don't claim to be good cooks claim to be great grillers. It's pervasive. My cousin Ricardo rarely cooks anything but if there's a fire to be made he's the first one there with the match and the tongs. People love fire, love to cook over fire and love to eat food that has been cooked over a fire.

Grilling on the barbecue is simple, and there is only one absolute rule: don't just turn everything to high. High heat, low heat, indirect heat—all effect the food in different ways. Learn how to use the heat.

BARBECUE

OBEDIENT INGREDIENT

Papaya

PAPAYA BARBECUE CHICKEN *served with* COCONUT RICE *&* WATERCRESS PAPAYA SALAD

Serves 4

I grew up with papaya. It's often served at the end of a meal to help with digestion and to offer something cool and sweet in hot climates. Flavour-wise, the **papaya barbecue sauce** still has the balance of sweet and sour, with the tanginess you expect from a barbecue sauce, but the base flavour profile is distinctly papaya. Instead of the fruit being cooked into a chutney it plays a starring role.

The **chicken** will need a good 12 to 15 minutes at a low-medium heat to cook through. Anything higher will cause it to burn. Don't move it around, don't fiddle. Just let it do its thing.

I like to use **coconut rice** to introduce new flavours to kids and others who aren't so adventurous and are wary of coconut milk. They love this rice once they taste it. Coconut rice adds flavour to something without a confrontation. It's a really nice surprise for adults who don't see any visual cues that there's a different flavour in the rice.

When you're eating barbecued food it's nice to have a salad for the contrast of flavour and texture. A salad never has to be dull. This quick salad has something different—watercress. The watercress-papaya combo aids digestion— it's a meal that just makes you feel good. You can mix your greens, or add or substitute pea sprouts, red romaine or butter lettuce—whatever you have on hand.

Papaya Marinade for Chicken

¼ cup (60 mL) coconut cream from top
   of 1 can (reserve the rest for Coconut
   Rice) (full-fat works best in this recipe)
2 Tbsp (30 mL) cilantro stems, chopped
1 clove garlic, minced
1 Tbsp (15 mL) ginger, minced
Seeds of 1 large papaya
Zest and juice of 1 lime
Zest and juice of 1 lemon

Combine all the ingredients in a bowl.

Papaya Barbecue Sauce

1 Tbsp (15 mL) vegetable oil
1 sweet onion, finely diced
¾ cup (185 mL) sugar
1 scotch bonnet pepper, pith and seeds
   removed, and quartered
Zest and juice of 2 limes
Zest and juice of 1 lemon
1 cup (250 mL) water
½ cup (125 mL) seasoned rice wine
   vinegar
5 cups (1.25 L) papaya flesh, large dice
2 tsp (10 mL) salt

Heat the oil in a pot over medium heat
and add the onion. Cook and stir the
onion until it becomes translucent but
not brown. Add the sugar, scotch bonnet
and lime and lemon zests. Stir, allowing
the sugar to dissolve. Add the water, the
lime and lemon juice and the vinegar.
Bring the mixture to a boil and stir well.
Add the papaya and season the mixture
with the salt. Bring it to a boil again, then
reduce the heat and allow it to simmer for
15 minutes. Transfer the sauce to a blender,
allow to cool for 4 minutes and purée
until smooth.

*Store in the refrigerator for up to three
days. Alternatively, store frozen in an airtight
container for up to two weeks.*

Grilled Chicken

4 marinated boneless skinless chicken
   breasts
Papaya Marinade for Chicken
1 Tbsp (15 mL) vegetable oil
½ cup (125 mL) Papaya Barbecue Sauce
¼ cup (60 mL) Spiced Cashew Nuts
   (see page 156), coarsely chopped
1 Tbsp (15 mL) cilantro leaves (optional
   garnish)

Immerse the chicken in the marinade
and place in the fridge to marinate for a
minimum of 1 hour, up to a maximum of
24 hours.

Heat the grill to low medium heat and
brush with the oil. Remove the chicken
from the marinade and place it on the grill.
Baste each chicken breast with 2 Tbsp
(30 mL) of the papaya barbecue sauce.
Continue basting it occasionally until the
chicken is cooked through, 12 to 15 minutes, making sure to flip the chicken 3 or
4 times throughout the cooking process.

Garnish the grilled chicken with
chopped spiced cashews and cilantro
leaves.

Coconut Rice

1 tsp (5 mL) vegetable oil
1 tsp (5 mL) fennel seeds
1 tsp (5 mL) coriander seeds
2 cups (500 mL) jasmine rice
3 cups coconut milk (reduced fat if
   you prefer)
1 cup (250 mL) water
1 Tbsp (15 mL) sugar

Heat the vegetable oil in a medium pot
over medium heat. Add the fennel and
coriander seeds and toast. Add the rice
and stir to incorporate with the seeds.
Add the coconut milk, water and the sugar.
Bring the rice to a boil then reduce the
heat to a simmer and cover the pot. Cook
for 30 minutes, until the rice has absorbed
all the liquid and is cooked through. Fluff
the coconut milk rice with a fork.

> Instead of boring you with another version of chicken with barbecue sauce I'm raising the bar with our obedient ingredient—papaya. Papaya chicken is of my most popular recipes in terms of fan response. This is the most commonly tried recipe, and the first one mastered by almost everyone on the production crew.

Shallot Rice Wine Vinaigrette

2 Tbsp (30 mL) seasoned rice wine
    vinegar
1 Tbsp (15 mL) white wine vinegar
1 shallot, finely diced
Salt
¼ cup (60 mL) vegetable oil

In a small bowl, add the seasoned rice wine vinegar and white wine vinegar. Add the shallot and a pinch of salt and stir. Add the oil and mix with a fork. Season to taste.

Store in an airtight container refrigerated for up to three days.

Watercress and Papaya Salad

2 small ripe papayas, peeled, cut in half
    and sliced 1 inch (2.5 cm) thick
1 bunch watercress, thick stems removed,
    rinsed and dried
Shallot Rice Wine Vinaigrette
¼ cup (60 mL) Spiced Cashew Nuts
    (see page 156), whole

Arrange the sliced papaya on a plate and pile the watercress on top. Drizzle the watercress salad with the vinaigrette and whole spiced cashews.

Fermented Black Beans

GRILLED STEAK *served with* BLACK BEAN SHRIMP *&* ROASTED EGGPLANT *&* BROCCOLI DUST

Serves 4

This meal starts with **black bean sauce** as a base: add the **shrimp**, and spoon it over the steak for a whole new approach. Black bean sauce is a Chinese pantry staple and popular for beef, shrimp and chicken on take-out menus.

Fermented black beans are very inexpensive. Go to any Chinese grocery store and you'll find that a big box of black beans costs about a dollar or two. You can make dozens of portions from that one box. Black beans have the consistency of a densely packed jellybean and a rich, deep, earthy, salty caramel flavour.

Roasted eggplant works as not only as a vegetable complement to the **broccoli dust** in this meal but also as a little something extra to sop up that delicious black bean sauce.

Broccoli dust is a delicate, elegant, restaurant-worthy way to serve broccoli, which also works well at home. Shave the broccoli buds, then finely dice and sauté the soft part of the stalks, adding the buds just for a few seconds at the end of the cooking process. Sprinkle the broccoli dust around the plate for colour and texture.

This recipe is a good transition for those who don't like to cook but like to grill. With this recipe you cook like a real chef.

Black Bean Sauce

1 tsp (5 mL) vegetable oil

2 cloves garlic, minced

1 shallot, minced

1 Tbsp (15 mL) ginger, minced

¼ cup + 1 Tbsp (75 mL) fermented black
    beans, roughly chopped

1 red finger chili, with seeds, minced

½ cup (125 mL) soy sauce

¼ cup (60 mL) water

¼ cup (60 mL) seasoned rice wine vinegar

1 Tbsp (15 mL) sugar

1½ tsp (2.5 mL) cornstarch mixed with
    1 Tbsp (15 mL) water

2 cilantro stems, finely chopped

Heat the vegetable oil in a large sauté
pan over medium to high heat. Add the
garlic, shallot and ginger and sauté until
golden and tender. Add the fermented
black beans and chili and stir to incorporate. Add the soy sauce, ¼ cup (60 mL)
water, the seasoned rice wine vinegar and
the sugar and stir. Add the cornstarch
and water mixture to the pan, stir and
allow the black bean sauce to thicken for
1 minute before removing it from the heat.
Add the cilantro stems, stir and set aside.

Use all of the sauce for this meal right
away as it does not reheat well.

*Store in an airtight container refrigerated
for up to three days.*

Roasted Eggplant

1 eggplant, cut into 1-inch (2.5 cm) circles

3 Tbsp (45 mL) vegetable oil

Salt

Pepper

Preheat the oven to 400°F (200°C) and
line a baking tray with parchment paper.

Place the eggplant pieces on the baking
tray and pierce them with a fork. Drizzle
the oil over the eggplant and season with
salt and pepper. Roast in the oven until

> "Mixing meat and fish, otherwise known as "surf and turf,"
> emerged from California as a restaurant trend, but every
> culture with a mixed farming and fishing tradition has its
> own "surf and turf." The fun part of this recipe is adding the
> shrimp (the surf), to the steak (the turf) by means of the Black
> Bean Shrimp sauce. This is a crew favourite. They devoured
> the whole dish before the photo session for the meal was over
> and most of the team made this at home for their families.

the eggplant is slightly caramelized and
tender, approximately 20 minutes.

Grilled Steak

1 Tbsp (15 mL) vegetable oil

Four 6–8 oz (230 g) pieces of beef
    tenderloin (trussed, optional)

Pepper

Preheat to medium and lightly oil the grill.

Season the steaks with pepper and
place them on the grill, turning them
over halfway through cooking. Cook the
steak to the desired doneness. Remove the
steaks from the grill and allow them to
rest, tented, for 5 minutes before serving.

Broccoli Dust

½ Tbsp (7.5 mL) butter

½ tsp (2.5 mL) vegetable oil

1 shallot, minced

1 clove garlic, minced

2 heads of broccoli, florets shaved, stalks
    finely diced

Salt

Pepper

Heat the butter and vegetable oil in a sauté
pan over medium heat. Add the shallot
and garlic and sauté until caramelized
and tender. Add the diced broccoli stalks,
and stir to incorporate. Once the broccoli

stems are tender, add the shaved florets
and season with salt and pepper. Stir the
broccoli dust, remove the pan from the
heat and set aside.

Black Bean Shrimp

1 Tbsp (15 mL) vegetable oil

1 shallot, minced

12 large shrimp, shells removed, deveined
    and roughly chopped

1½ cups (375 mL) Black Bean Sauce

2 green onions, sliced

½ cup (125 mL) roughly chopped cilantro
    leaves

Heat the vegetable oil in a small sauté pan.
Add the shallot and sauté until tender.
Add the shrimp and stir. Once the shrimp
is cooked, add the black bean sauce. Stir
the black bean shrimp and remove the
pan from the heat. Add the green onion
and cilantro leaves and set aside until
assembly.

**Place three pieces of the roasted egg-
plant on each plate. Place one of the
rested grilled steaks on top of each of
the roasted eggplants. Spoon the black
bean shrimp over the grilled steaks,
then garnish with spoonfuls of broccoli
dust around the outside of the plates.**

OBEDIENT INGREDIENT

Tahini

TAHINI GRILLED SALMON *with* SAUTÉED SPINACH & BEETS *with* SESAME SEEDS & EGGPLANT PURÉE & TAHINI SAUCE

Serves 4

Tahini is ground white sesame seed paste. Its combined mild and bitter flavour has a distinct sesame sweetness, and it tints the salmon with a subtle, bittersweet taste.

If you like the crispy skin as part of **salmon**, leave it on; if not, you can use it to make an amazing garnish that adds a rich crunch.

The **beets with sesame seeds** are the starch in this meal. Most people enjoy beets when beets are offered but don't cook them because they aren't sure really what to do with them and they're afraid their hands and kitchen will get stained.

Boil beets with salted, sugared water with a bit of vinegar.

The sugar bumps up the natural sweetness in the beet; the salt bumps up all the natural flavour and gives it a savoury tinge. The vinegar helps preserve the colour, so you get a clean, vibrant-looking beet.

I use gloves when I peel beets but a clean old rag that you don't mind getting stained also works. It's best to peel beets when they're warm as the skin comes off very easily then and yes—it's a messy job, so peel them into a bowl instead of your countertop.

Eggplant purée with tahini builds on the bittersweet of sesame. It's a very simple dish and works so well with the flavours of salmon and spinach. You can also use it as a dip or on bread.

Crispy Salmon Skin

Reserved salmon skin

Salt

Pepper

Preheat the grill to medium-high. Season the salmon skin with salt and pepper and place it on the grill, outside skin down. Once the skin begins to bubble, flip it and grill until the salmon skin is completely crisp. Transfer the crispy salmon skin to a paper towel. Cut the crispy salmon skin in half and set it aside until you're ready to garnish the tahini grilled salmon.

Sautéed Spinach

1 Tbsp (15 mL) olive oil

1 clove garlic, minced

1 shallot, minced

1 bunch spinach, stems removed and washed

Salt

Pepper

Heat the olive oil in a sauté pan over medium heat. Once the oil is hot, add the garlic and shallot and sauté until tender. Add the spinach and toss to incorporate until it has wilted. Season the sautéed spinach with salt and pepper and remove from the heat.

Beets with Sesame Seeds

3 large beets

¼ cup (60 mL) red wine vinegar

2 Tbsp (30 mL) salt

2 Tbsp (30 mL) sugar

1 cup (250 mL) sesame seeds

Place the beets, vinegar, salt and sugar in a pot filled with cold water. Bring the water to a boil then immediately reduce it to a simmer and cook until the beets are tender, approximately 15 to 20 minutes.

Wearing gloves, remove the skins of the beets, dice them into bite-sized pieces and allow them to cool to room temperature. Place the sesame seeds in a bowl and roll the beets in them in preparation for serving. Set aside for assembly.

Eggplant Purée

2 large eggplants cut in half lengthwise, flesh scored

⅓ cup (80 mL) tahini

2 Tbsp (30 mL) olive oil

Salt

Pepper

Preheat the oven to 375°F (190°C) and line a baking tray with parchment paper.

Place the eggplants skin side up on the tray and roast until caramelized and cooked, approximately 30 minutes. Remove the eggplants from the oven and scoop the flesh into a food processor. Add the tahini and olive oil and purée until smooth. Season to taste with salt and pepper.

Tahini Sauce

½ cup (125 mL) sour cream (reduced fat if you prefer)

⅓ cup (80 mL) 2% milk

¼ cup (60 mL) tahini

Juice of ½ lemon

1 Tbsp (15 mL) honey

½ tsp (2.5 mL) sesame oil

Salt to taste

Place all the ingredients in a bowl and stir to incorporate. Cover and place in the fridge until ready to serve.

Store in an airtight container refrigerated for up to two days.

Tahini Grilled Salmon

1 Tbsp (15 mL) vegetable oil

¼ cup (60 mL) tahini

1 tsp (5 mL) soy sauce

One 20 oz (600 g) salmon fillet, cut into 5 oz (150 g) portions, skin removed and reserved

Preheat the grill to medium and lightly oil it with the vegetable oil. Mix the tahini and soy sauce in a bowl. Brush the salmon on both sides with the tahini soy sauce mixture and place it on the grill. Cook for approximately 3 minutes on each side then remove from the grill. Transfer the salmon to a room temperature plate and tent with foil to keep warm until ready to serve the meal.

Spoon the eggplant purée in the centre of a plate and place the sautéed spinach on top. Place the tahini grilled salmon over the sautéed spinach then drizzle the tahini sauce around the centre of the dish. Scatter the beets with sesame seeds around the plate. Garnish with the crispy salmon skin.

" Salmon is good for the grill because it is firm and holds together. It's a good fish to practise your grilling on because its marbled fattiness makes it quite forgiving.

For this recipe, the salmon is given a tahini rub before grilling.

Passion Fruit

GRILLED PASSION FRUIT PORK SATAYS *served with* PASSION FRUIT TZATZIKI & HERBED COUSCOUS & VEGETABLE STIR-FRY

Serves 4

Passion fruit is the base of the marinade for these **pork satays** and I also add a little of it to **tzatziki** for flavour. Its crunchy seeds are edible as well as fun to eat. Its tangy bite adds to the more traditional lemon juice in the tzatziki. Its acid gets into the pork and its hint of sour nicely balances the tzatziki's creaminess. The marinade works well with white meats, but I wouldn't recommend it for beef.

The secret to a good **stir-fry** is to chop everything ahead of time. Have all the ingredients laid out because once you start cooking it all goes super-fast. You don't want to overcook your vegetables or they go mushy. Chinese food demands the freshest produce so that everything maintains its crispy freshness when served steaming hot. You want the vegetables heated through but crisp and at their peak of freshness.

For the **herbed coucous**, we've added Mediterranean herbs—thyme and oregano—but you can easily switch up the herbs to match the main course. For an Italian-inspired meal, basil and oregano would be delicious.

"This is totally inspired by my Greek friends. I have this whole Greek crew I love. They're big and loud and passionate and generous. When I go visit they're often roasting two pigs on the spit. I never leave hungry.

This dish honours the Greek tradition of kabobs and tzatziki. But when you get right down to it, it's meat on a stick over a fire. Primal.

Grilled Passion Fruit Pork Satays

One 3–4 lb (1.5–1.8 kg) boneless pork
   shoulder, trimmed and cut into 1-inch
   (2.5 cm) cubes
2 passion fruits, pulp and seeds only,
   shell discarded
1 shallot, minced
¼ cup (60 mL) basil, finely chopped
¼ cup (60 mL) coconut milk (reduced fat
   if you prefer)
1 Tbsp (15 mL) black pepper
Salt
Skewers

Place all the ingredients, except the salt, in a dish and mix well to ensure that the pork is coated in the marinade and that everything is evenly combined. Place the pork in the fridge to marinate for a minimum of 30 minutes, to a maximum of 24 hours.

When you are ready to serve, preheat the grill to medium.

Remove the marinated pork from the fridge. Place approximately 5 pieces of pork on each skewer. Season the pork with salt and place the satays on the grill. Grill the pork on all sides; total cooking time is roughly 6 minutes. Once the pork satays are charred and cooked through, remove from the heat and set aside for assembly.

Passion Fruit Tzatziki

2 passion fruits, pulp and seeds only,
   shell discarded
1 cup (250 mL) cream cheese
½ cup (125 mL) basil, finely chopped
¼ cup (60 mL) whole milk
1 shallot, minced
Juice of ½ lemon
Salt to taste
Black pepper to taste

Place the pulp (including seeds) of one passion fruit and the remaining ingredients in a bowl and mix to incorporate. Spoon the remaining passion fruit pulp (including seeds) overtop. Cover the passion fruit tzatziki and place it in the fridge until ready to serve.

Store in an airtight container refrigerated for up to three days.

Herbed Couscous

1½ cups (375 mL) couscous
¼ cup (60 mL) olive oil
Salt
1½ cups (375 mL) boiled water
½ cup (125 mL) roughly chopped oregano
2 Tbsp (30 mL) roughly chopped thyme

In a large bowl, add the couscous, olive oil and salt to taste. Pour the boiled water over the couscous and cover the bowl with plastic wrap. Once the couscous has absorbed all the water, approximately 15 minutes, remove the plastic wrap and fluff with a fork. Add the herbs and fluff once again to incorporate, then set the couscous aside until ready to serve.

Vegetable Stir-Fry

1 Tbsp (15 mL) vegetable oil
1 clove garlic, thinly sliced
1 can whole baby corn, drained and rinsed
2 carrots, peeled and thinly sliced on a
   bias
2 cups (500 mL) snow peas, cleaned and
   ends trimmed
½ red onion, julienned
1 tsp (5 mL) sesame oil
Salt

Heat the vegetable oil in a large sauté pan or wok over medium heat. Add the garlic and toss until golden brown. Add the baby corn, carrots, snow peas and onion and toss until the vegetables are tender. Add the sesame oil, season with salt and remove the pan from the heat.

Spoon the herbed couscous in the centre of a plate. Scatter the vegetable stir-fry around the herbed couscous and place the passion fruit marinated pork satays on top of the herbed couscous. Serve with the passion fruit tzatziki.

OBEDIENT INGREDIENT

Tamarind

LAMB KABOBS *with* TAMARIND SAUCE *&*
BLACK-EYED PEAS *&* RICE

Serves 4

Generally with meats such as **lamb** I like to add a citrus or acidic flavour to cut the fattiness, and tamarind works really well. The **tamarind sauce** is very easy. Toss everything in the pot, cook it down, strain it, and it's done.

The **marinade** is oil-based with the rudiments of onions, garlic, shallot and pepper—but no salt. We don't want to draw any moisture from the meat.

For a successful **kabob**, cut the meat in equal-sized pieces so it all cooks evenly and use a low-medium heat. Don't fuss with it too much—turn it once it has marks and it's good to go. If you want to know if it's cooked, cut a little piece off and bite it.

In the Caribbean, **peas and rice** is a dinner staple. To keep this recipe simple, I use canned **black-eyed peas**. Although I know that many grannies will be rolling in their graves at my suggestion, this recipe is a good one with which to start your peas and rice journey. Once you get more confident you can graduate to dried black-eyed peas, which require soaking overnight and adding more water.

Why do we use mint with lamb? Lamb can be paired with other strong flavours such as citrus and fragrant spices but mint with lamb has proven over time to be one of the most flavourful food combinations.

Tamarind Sauce

1 tsp (5 mL) coriander seed

½ cinnamon stick

One 14 oz (400 mL) can of coconut milk
    (reduced fat is not an option here)

Two 7 oz (200 g) packages of tamarind

1½ cups (375 mL) water

½ cup (125 mL) sugar

Juice of 1 grapefruit

½ Tbsp (7.5 mL) ginger, smashed

Salt to taste

Pepper to taste

Place the coriander seed and cinnamon stick in a pot and toast over medium heat for 1 minute. Add the remaining ingredients, except salt and pepper, breaking up the tamarind with a spoon, and stir. Bring to a boil, then reduce to a simmer. Cook the tamarind sauce, uncovered, for 15 to 20 minutes until thickened. Strain the sauce through a fine mesh sieve into a bowl and season to taste.

Store in an airtight container for up to one week.

Lamb Marinade

1 shallot, diced

1 clove garlic, finely chopped

2 Tbsp (30 mL) vegetable oil

1 Tbsp (15 mL) black pepper

½ Tbsp (7.5 mL) ginger, finely chopped

Combine all the ingredients in a bowl.

Lamb Kabobs

2 lb (1 kg) lamb leg, silverskin removed,
    cut into 1-inch (2.5 cm) pieces

Lamb Marinade

1 medium red onion, inner core removed
    and reserved, outer layers cut into
    1- × 1-inch (2.5 × 2.5 cm) pieces

1 bunch mint

Salt

Skewers

Marinate the lamb in the marinade for a minimum of 30 minutes, to a maximum of 24 hours.

Heat the grill to medium.

To assemble the lamb kabobs, push one piece of the red onion through the skewer. Then push one piece of lamb through the skewer so that the lamb is resting on the red onion. Skewer the mint, stem and leaves, wrapping it around the red onion and the lamb. Continue to push the lamb and red onions through the skewers, while wrapping with mint stem with leaves. Repeat this process until all the skewers are full.

Grill the lamb kabobs until the lamb is medium rare, approximately 10 to 12 minutes.

Serve with the tamarind sauce.

Black-Eyed Peas and Rice

1 tsp (5 mL) vegetable oil

Inner core of medium red onion, from lamb
    kabobs recipe, finely diced

3 cloves garlic, minced

Salt

Pepper

1¼ cups (310 mL) parboiled long-grain
    white rice

One 19 oz (540 mL) can of black-eyed peas,
    rinsed and drained

2¼ cups (560 mL) water

1 bunch mint, leaves picked

Heat the vegetable oil in a pot to taste over medium to high heat. Add the red onion and garlic and cook until translucent. Season with salt and pepper. Add the rice and stir.

Add water, stir and bring to a boil. Reduce the heat to a simmer and cover the pot with a lid. Simmer for 15 minutes until the rice is cooked. Add the black-eyed peas towards the last 5 minutes of cooking and cover the pot again. Transfer the black-eyed peas and rice to a bowl, cool slightly and garnish with mint.

Place peas and rice on a plate and rest one or two skewers on top of the rice. Drizzle the kabobs with tamarind sauce or serve on the side for easy dipping.

> " When I was growing up in the Caribbean we had a tamarind tree in our yard. I used to love picking the large brown fuzzy pods and stripping away the shells to get at the sticky paste around the seeds inside. Now you can buy tamarind as a shrink-wrapped paste that you can add to a liquid, cook down and then strain, while retaining all the beautiful tamarind flavour.

Pasta is one of those foods that is both highbrow and lowbrow. It is a staple of our budget-conscious days but also a feature in fancy Italian restaurants. Ironic, eh? But food irony is the best kind because at least we can eat our own words and smile about it.

To salt the water or not to salt the water? A great debate. Some say never salt the water. Some say salt it to add flavour to the pasta. In some parts of the world they cook the pasta in seawater. Me, I like to salt, always with kosher salt, because I love the taste of well-seasoned food. It's your choice.

However, do not add oil to the water—ever. If you are worried about the pasta sticking together, use an ample amount of water—a ratio of at least four parts water to one part pasta—and leave lots of space in the pot.

The desired texture of pasta is a personal preference in so many ways. Purists like it al dente, with a bit of bite to it. My wife likes it mushy, although I'm trying to convince her otherwise. The best way to find the right texture for you is to test as you go.

It's always best to finish pasta in a pan on the burner. Get the sauce warmed up, pick up the cooked, drained pasta with the tongs, get it all coated with the sauce. Then it's straight onto the plate and right to the table, nice and hot. Freshly grated Parmesan or shaved Asiago is always a nice final touch.

PASTA

Wonton

WONTON RAVIOLI *with* APPLE CIDER GLAZE *served with* CARROT *&* FENNEL SALAD *with* WHITE WINE DRESSING

Serves 4

Wonton wrappers can be square or circular, vary in thickness and can be filled with almost anything sweet or savoury. The thickness of the wrapper affects how much you can stuff in them, and how long you have to cook them. Do a test run to get your times right or just taste as you go. An egg wash helps the wonton wrapper stick together so that the filling doesn't pop out. The trick is to press out the air before you fully seal the wrapper.

Drizzle the **apple cider glaze** over the ravioli to add a bit of taste and, of course, a sauce. All pasta needs a good sauce. Alternatively, toss the pasta with some olive oil and chives—easy.

Italian food makes good use of fennel, and I wanted to tie that flavour back in to the meal, hence the **carrot and fennel salad**. Warming the dressing gives the flavours impact. Soak the raisins overnight in white wine and they'll plump up and be full of the flavour of the wine.

Apple Cider Glaze

4 cups (1 L) non-alcoholic apple cider

1½ tsp (2.5 mL) freshly ground black
    pepper

Place the apple cider in a large sauté pan
over high heat. Once it has reduced by
half and has achieved a thick syrup consistency, add the black pepper, stir and
set aside. Keep on the lowest temperature,
covered, to keep warm.

Wonton Ravioli

½ lb (250 g) ground turkey

½ lb (250 g) ground pork

½ cup (125 mL) finely grated Asiago
    cheese

2 cloves garlic, minced

1 shallot, minced

2 Tbsp (30 mL) roughly chopped fresh
    sage

1 tsp (5 mL) freshly ground pepper

One 16 oz (454 g) round wonton wrappers
    (60 wonton wrappers)

1 egg, whisked for egg wash

Apple Cider Glaze

¼ cup (60 mL) finely chopped chives

Salt

In a tall, rimmed sauté pan bring heavily
salted water to a boil. Reduce the heat
slightly to a gentle boil.

Meanwhile, place the turkey, pork, Asiago cheese, garlic, shallot, sage and pepper
in a bowl and mix well to incorporate.

To assemble the wonton ravioli, place
a wonton wrapper on a clean, dry work
surface and brush the entire wrapper with
egg wash. Keep the remaining wonton
wrappers covered while you work to prevent them from drying out. Place 1 Tbsp
(15 mL) of meat mixture in the centre of
the wonton wrapper.

To cover, gently stretch another wonton overtop, connecting the edges of the

wrappers and pressing to secure. Gently
lift the ravioli, cupping your hands over
the filling to release any air inside, then
pinch around rim to secure the wonton
and place it on a dry tray. Repeat with the
remaining wontons.

To cook, gently place five wontons in
the boiling water, stirring frequently, until
the meat is cooked and no longer pink,
approximately 3 to 5 minutes.

To serve, place the wonton ravioli in a
large bowl, drizzle with apple cider glaze
until all wontons are coated evenly, place
on a serving dish and garnish with the
chopped chives.

Makes 30 wontons.

Carrot and Fennel Salad with White Wine Dressing

½ cup (125 mL) sultana raisins

1 cup (250 mL) dry white wine

2 Tbsp (30 mL) honey

2 carrots, peeled and cut into ribbons
    with peeler

½ fennel, thinly sliced

1½ Tbsp (22.5 mL) capers, drained

1¼ cups (310 mL) fresh parsley, roughly
    chopped

½ cup (125 mL) sliced almonds, toasted

Place the raisins in a bowl and soak them
in the white wine for 1 hour or overnight.
Drain and reserve the white wine.

Place the reserved white wine in a small

"This recipe is very dear
to our hearts here at
Everyday Exotic, because it
is the recipe we shot in our
demo for Food Network
Canada before we went
on air. When we got to our
second season, we all—the
crew and the producers—
wanted to do the recipe
again, and as fate would
have it, the recipe was both
the very first one and the
very last one we shot.

It's a quick way to make
fresh ravioli at home,
especially when you use
premade wonton wrappers.
It was and still is the
perfect recipe to showcase
Everyday Exotic.

Originally I used chicken.
It works well, but turkey is
leaner and the fat from the
cheese stops it from being
too dry.

pot, add the honey and cook over medium-
high heat until the liquid reduces to ⅓ cup
(80 mL), approximately 5 minutes.

Place the carrots, fennel, capers and
soaked raisins in a large bowl.

Pour the white wine dressing over the
carrot and fennel salad, add the chopped
parsley and toasted almonds, toss and
serve.

King Oyster Mushroom

FETTUCCINE *with* KING OYSTER MUSHROOMS *&*
KING OYSTER BRUSCHETTA

Serves 4

The **king oyster mushroom** provides a safe introduction to the wide world of mushrooms beyond the very common button mushroom and the mighty portobello. For a giant step forward, try the trumpets, creminis and shiitake.

This is a rich, creamy pasta like an alfredo. The mushrooms make it hearty and flavourful. A lot of people don't know how to make a mushroom pasta so they get a can of mushroom soup, bring it to the boil and add their cooked pasta.

Once you've entered the world of mushrooms you can experiment with different varieties and then move on to finish with lemon thyme instead of regular thyme, or add shrimp and tarragon. The principles stay the same, you just swap out the ingredients.

Serving more than one starch in a meal is common in a lot of cultures, and here we have pasta with **bruschetta**. The bruschetta works well as a side to almost any dish. It's simple and a good testament to the concept that tasty does not have to be complicated. Just as the mushrooms are cooling down, add the goat cheese; it will start to melt and bind everything together.

King Oyster Fettuccine

One 16 oz (450 g) package of fettuccine

¼ cup (60 mL) butter

2 Tbsp (30 mL) olive oil

3 cloves garlic, minced

2 shallots, diced

5 king oyster mushrooms, roughly
   chopped

1 tsp (5 mL) picked leaves of fresh thyme

¼ cup (60 mL) dry white wine

½ cup (125 mL) 35% cream

2 cups (500 mL) baby spinach

1 cup (250 mL) chopped chives (cut into
   1-inch/2.5 cm pieces)

Salt

Pepper

Cook the pasta according to the package
directions.

Heat the butter and olive oil in a sauté
pan over medium-high heat. Sauté the
garlic and shallots until light brown. Add
the mushrooms and thyme, and sauté
until the mushrooms are golden brown.
Deglaze with the white wine and stir. Add
the cream and stir.

Allow the sauce to reduce until it
becomes thick enough to coat the back
of a spoon. Add the spinach and toss to
combine.

Transfer the cooked, drained pasta to
the sauté pan with the sauce and toss to
coat. Add the chives, toss, season with salt
and pepper and remove from the heat.

King Oyster Bruschetta

3 Tbsp (45 mL) olive oil

1 bunch green onions, white bottoms and
   green tops separated and chopped

3 cloves garlic, chopped

2 tsp (10 mL) fresh thyme leaves

4 king oyster mushrooms, large dice

1 Tbsp (15 mL) soy sauce

Salt

Pepper

½ cup (125 mL) goat cheese

1 baguette, cut into 1-inch (2.5 cm) slices
   and lightly toasted

Preheat oven to broil (high setting if your
oven has one) and line a baking tray with
parchment paper.

Heat the oil in a sauté pan over
medium-high heat. Add the green onion
whites, garlic and thyme, and sauté until
light golden brown. Add the mushrooms
and sauté until golden brown. Add the
soy sauce and continue to cook until
the liquid is nearly completely reduced,
roughly 1 minute. Add the chopped green
onion tops, season with salt and pepper,
then remove from the heat. Transfer to a
bowl and allow to cool slightly. Add the

goat cheese to the mushroom mixture and
mix to incorporate.

Place the baguette slices on the lined
baking tray and spoon the mushroom mixture overtop. Broil until the cheese has
softened, approximately 3 minutes.

OBEDIENT INGREDIENT

Pine Nuts

PINE NUT LAMB MEATBALLS *with* PASTA & PINE NUT BREAD SALAD

Serves 4

At a good Italian restaurant, the **meatballs** will be soft and tender. Part of the reason for this is the high quality of the meat that is used, but often some shredded, soaked bread is added to soften the meatball. This recipe uses Italian ciabatta, soaked in milk.

I like the hand-squeeze method of forming meatballs. Grab some of the meat mix, squeeze it, see what pops out of the top of your hand—and that's the meatball. You can re-size any of the meatballs that need to be brought into line with the others.

Serve this with a very basic tomato sauce, finished with a nice cheese and a drizzle of good olive oil. I like to shave

Parmesan cheese with a vegetable peeler to create nice long ribbons right at the last minute. It looks good, and the hunks of cheese can be broken up or eaten individually.

Pine nut bread salad is a take on the classic bread salad known to Italians as panzanella. I've added pine nuts to this recipe. Start with bread that is starting to go crusty and add some nice olive oil and roasted cherry tomatoes. The torn basil, parsley and chives add so much fresh flavour.

Think of this as a revisited take on pasta and salad that uses all the classic elements and makes a quick weekday meal.

Pine Nut Lamb Meatballs

1½ cups (375 mL) ciabatta, crusts removed
    and shredded
½ cup (125 mL) whole milk
1¼ lb (625 g) ground lamb
½ cup (125 mL) pine nuts, toasted
⅓ cup (80 mL) dried currants
2 shallots, minced
1 clove garlic, minced
1 egg
1½ Tbsp (22.5 mL) thyme, chopped
1 Tbsp (15 mL) olive oil + extra for frying
1 tsp (5 mL) black pepper
Salt to taste

Place the shredded pieces of bread in a
small bowl, cover with milk and soak until
the bread is soft, approximately 10 minutes.

Place the remaining ingredients in
a large bowl with the bread and mix
thoroughly with your hands, being careful
not to overmix. Form meatballs with your
hands and place them on a large plate or
baking tray.

Heat oil in a cast-iron pan over
medium-high heat, add the meatballs and
fry until the meat has browned, making
sure to brown all sides evenly. Remove
from the heat.

Makes approximately 24 meatballs.

Pasta Sauce

2 Tbsp (30 mL) vegetable oil
3 cloves garlic, minced
1 sprig rosemary
One 28 oz (796 ml) can whole tomatoes
1 bay leaf
Salt
Pepper
Pine Nut Lamb Meatballs
One 17.5 oz (500 g) package of fettuccine
¼ cup (60 mL) Parmesan cheese, shaved
    into ribbons with vegetable peeler
¼ cup (60 mL) parsley, roughly chopped

Preheat the oven to 375°F (190°C).

Heat the oil in a large, wide-mouthed,
ovenproof pan over medium-high heat,
then add the garlic and rosemary to infuse
the oil. Once the garlic has caramelized,
add the tomatoes and bay leaf, stir and
season with salt and pepper. Add the
meatballs to the tomato sauce, and transfer to the oven until the tomato sauce
has reduced slightly, approximately
30 minutes.

To serve, place the pasta in the centre
of a plate, spoon tomato sauce overtop and
allow six meatballs per serving.

Garnish with Parmesan cheese and
parsley.

Pine Nut Bread Salad

1½ cups (375 mL) ciabatta, crusts
    removed, cut into ½-inch- (1 cm) thick
    slices
4 Tbsp (60 mL) olive oil
Salt
Pepper
1 sprig thyme
1 sprig rosemary
1 pint cherry tomatoes
½ cup (125 mL) pine nuts, toasted
¼ cup (60 mL) julienned red onions
1 Tbsp (15 mL) aged balsamic vinegar
2 Tbsp (30 mL) hand-torn basil leaves
2 Tbsp (30 mL) hand-torn parsley
2 Tbsp (30 mL) chopped chives (cut into
    1-inch/2.5 cm pieces)

Preheat the grill to medium heat.

Brush the bread slices sparingly with
3 Tbsp (45 mL) of the olive oil and season
with salt and pepper on both sides. Grill
the bread on both sides until golden and
crisp, remove from the heat, cut into 1-inch
(2.5 cm) cubes and place in a large bowl.

Heat the remaining oil in a large pan
over medium heat then add the thyme and
rosemary sprigs to infuse the oil. Add the
tomatoes to the pan, toss until the skins
split and become slightly charred, then
place in the bowl with the bread. Add the
toasted pine nuts, red onions and balsamic
vinegar and season with salt and pepper.

Garnish with basil, parsley and chives,
toss together gently and serve.

> " I think just about everyone
> has a favourite meatball
> recipe. I'm using lamb in
> this recipe for its familiar
> texture and flair. The pine
> nuts amp up the texture.

OBEDIENT INGREDIENT

Rapini

VEGETABLE LASAGNA *with* HOMEMADE PASTA *&* JALAPEÑO BECHAMEL *&* CHARRED RAPINI

Serves 4

Béchamel is a classic white sauce, but to take it up a notch I add **jalapeño**, which tints it a light green that works well with the other colours of this dish, and adds a touch of heat. To make béchamel sauce you first make a roux, the classic French thickening agent that is one part flour and one part fat. Adding milk to the roux makes it a béchamel.

In this **lasagna**, tomato is not the base of the sauce, but one of the vegetables. Squeeze it by hand to break it up,

spread it around and remove some of the liquid. The real sauce in this lasagna is the jalapeño béchamel.

Why **rapini**? It has a vibrant green colour and when it's charred it adds a lot of substance and flavour. Its bitterness and sharpness is balanced out by a little drizzle of the **chili honey**.

Homemade Pasta

4 cups (1 L) all-purpose flour, + extra for
    dusting
1 tsp (5 mL) salt
6 large eggs, room temperature
1 Tbsp (15 mL) olive oil

Place the flour and salt in a large bowl
and make a well in the centre with your
hands. Place the eggs in the centre of the
well and gently incorporate the eggs into
the flour.

Dust a clean work surface with flour,
remove the dough from the bowl and
knead for approximately 5 minutes, until
the dough becomes smooth. Shape it into
a disc, wrap in plastic wrap and place in
the fridge for 30 minutes, to a maximum
of 48 hours.

Place a large pot of salted water over
high heat and bring to a boil.

Dust a clean work surface with flour,
remove the dough from the fridge, divide
into five equal pieces and cover with plastic wrap to prevent it from drying out.

Using a pasta machine, roll each piece
of dough out into long, thin pieces, place
on a tray and dust with flour. Repeat with
the remaining dough, dusting the pasta
with flour in between layers to prevent
sticking. Trim the sheets to fit your baking
dish if necessary.

Place the olive oil on a large baking
tray. Cook the pasta in boiling salted water
for approximately 3 to 4 minutes or until
al dente, remove gently, place on the oiled
tray, drizzle with oil to prevent from sticking and set aside.

*To store cooked pasta, lightly oil it and lay
it flat in an airtight container. Store refrigerated for up to three days.*

Roasted Squash Filling

2½ lb (250 g) butternut squash, peeled,
    seeds removed and cut into large dice
3 Tbsp (45 mL) olive oil
Salt
Pepper
1 Vidalia onion, diced
6 cloves garlic, chopped
2 Tbsp (30 mL) butter
¼ cup (60 mL) chopped fresh sage leaves

Preheat the oven to 400°F (200°C).

Place squash in a bowl, coat with 1 Tbsp
(15 mL) of olive oil and season with salt and
pepper. Roast the squash in the oven until
tender and caramelized, approximately
45 minutes, turning over halfway through
cooking. Remove from the oven, place in a
large bowl, mash slightly and set aside.

Heat the remaining olive oil in a sauté
pan over medium-high heat, add the onion
and garlic and sauté until golden brown.
Add the butter and allow to melt. Add the
sage, stir and remove from the heat. Add
to the roasted squash, season with salt and
pepper, gently fold and set aside.

Jalapeño Béchamel

¼ cup + 1 Tbsp (75 mL) butter
¼ cup + 1 Tbsp (75 mL) all-purpose flour
4 cups (1 L) scalded whole milk
3 jalapeños, cut in half, seeds removed
    and mashed in a mortar and pestle
Salt

Melt the butter in a small pot over
medium heat. Add the flour and stir with
a wooden spoon to incorporate the flour
into the butter until a paste consistency is
achieved. Add the scalded milk slowly and
in three separate additions, whisking constantly to incorporate smoothly, removing
all lumps. Once the mixture thickens, add
the mashed jalapeños, season with salt
and set aside.

*Store in an airtight container refrigerated
for up to three days.*

Vegetable Lasagna

1 Tbsp (15 mL) olive oil
1½ cups (375 mL) canned whole tomatoes,
    crushed by hands, juice reserved
10 sheets of pasta
Jalapeño Béchamel
1 bunch rapini, bottoms trimmed,
    blanched in salted water and roughly
    chopped
Roasted Squash Filling
2 cups (500 mL) ricotta cheese
½ cup (125 mL) Parmesan cheese, grated
¼ cup (60 mL) whole sage leaves, for
    garnish

Preheat the oven to 350°F (175°C). Oil a
9- × 13-inch (3.5 L) baking dish.

Layer the tomatoes, pasta, jalapeño
béchamel, chopped rapini, roasted squash
filling and ricotta, then sprinkle with the
parmesan. Repeat until you have used all
the ingredients, finishing with a layer of
béchamel. Place the whole sage leaves on
top, submerging them in sauce.

Bake in the oven for approximately
30 minutes, then broil for an additional
5 minutes until the jalapeño béchamel is
golden brown.

Chili Honey

3 Tbsp (45 mL) honey
1 tsp (5 mL) chili flakes
1 Tbsp (15 mL) dry white wine

Place the honey in a small pot over low heat until it has a thin consistency. Add the chili flakes, stir and remove from the heat.

Add the white wine, mix well and set aside.

Store in an airtight container refrigerated for up to one week.

Charred Rapini

1 bunch rapini, bottoms removed, blanched
    in salted water and roughly chopped
2 cups (500 mL) cipollini onions, cooked
    in boiling water until tender and peeled
3 Tbsp (45 mL) olive oil
2 cloves garlic, finely chopped
½ cup (125 mL) walnuts, toasted
Chili Honey

Preheat the grill to high.

In a bowl, lightly toss the rapini, cipollini onions, olive oil and garlic.

Place the rapini and onions on the grill, turning to ensure all sides are charred. Remove from the grill, place in a serving dish, garnish with the toasted walnuts and drizzle with the chili honey.

Serve charred rapini as a side dish to accompany the lasagna or any meal that needs a delicious green side vegetable.

"This is a good reference recipe for making pasta from scratch. Admittedly, it's a time-consuming activity, best done on a day off or a Sunday afternoon, but certainly worth the time.

Why do we love lasagna so much? When you see a nice big square of lasagna on your plate it's hard not to feel abundant. Who doesn't love cutting through the layers and experiencing all the flavours of a nice gooey lasagna? It's a great sit-down dinner food, and a great main for a self-serve dinner. And it tastes just as good, or even better, the next day.

I wanted to make a hearty vegetarian dish that all of my meat-eating buddies would like. I especially wanted Neil to like it. Neil is the go-to guy on our team who makes everything happen that needs to happen. He's a big guy and he has an even bigger appetite. His family owns a very successful sausage and cold cuts company so he has an allegiance to meat. The **roasted squash filling** rose to the challenge.

OBEDIENT INGREDIENT

Pistachio

PISTACHIO PESTO *with* ANGEL HAIR PASTA *&* ZUCCHINI GRATIN

Serves 4

Angel hair pasta is such a light pasta that it needs a very light sauce. Pesto, which is simply a mix of herbs and nuts with a bit of cheese, is perfect. A desire to experiment with the pistachio nut led me to create a light **pistachio pesto:** I swapped the pine nut of a classic pesto for pistachio, to change the flavour. In this case the experiment worked (unlike the one for my bacon cake!).

Whether eaten plain, seasoned red, shelled or not, pistachio nuts are buttery and decadent—two qualities that make them worthy of their own section in this book.

This pesto is so simple and so delicious that you may feel guilty. If you want to do some hard work for your dinner, put some real elbow grease into the mortar and pestle.

This pesto would also be off the hook drizzled on a steak, some chicken, or even tofu. You could also spread it on a piece of bread and grill it like you would an herbed foccaccia.

Since the main dish is so light you'll want to pair it up with a substantial side. Layer **zucchini**, onion, pesto and pistachios, and enjoy a lasagna-style gratin.

Pistachio Pesto

8 cups (2 L) basil leaves, washed and dried

1 cup (250 mL) olive oil

¾ cup (185 mL) unsalted pistachios, toasted and crushed in a mortar and pestle

½ cup (125 mL) grated Parmesan cheese

2 cloves garlic

Salt to taste

Pepper to taste

In batches, place the ingredients in a food processor and purée until smooth.

Remove the pistachio pesto from the blender and place in a container. Cover the top with 1 Tbsp (15 mL) of olive oil until ready to use.

Store refrigerated in an airtight container topped off with a little olive oil for up to one week.

Pistachio Pesto with Angel Hair Pasta

One 16 oz (454 g) package angel hair pasta

¼ cup (60 mL) pasta water, extra if needed

½ cup (125 mL) Pistachio Pesto

2 Tbsp (30 mL) olive oil

Salt

Pepper

1 cup (250 mL) cherry tomatoes halves

1 cup (250 mL) Parmesan cheese ribbons (shaved into ribbons with vegetable peeler)

¼ cup (60 mL) basil leaves

Cook the pasta according to the package directions, drain and reserve ¼ cup (60 mL) of the cooking water.

Heat a large sauté pan. Place the reserved pasta water, pistachio pesto and olive oil in the pan and toss to incorporate. Add the cooked angel hair pasta, gently fold into the pistachio pesto mixture and season with salt and pepper.

Divide among serving plates. Garnish with the cherry tomatoes, parmesan cheese, basil leaves and black pepper.

Zucchini Gratin

4 zucchini, tops trimmed, sliced lengthwise ¼-inch (6 mm) thick

½ cup (125 mL) Pistachio Pesto

2–3 ripe tomatoes, thinly sliced

1 Vidalia onion, sliced into thin rings

½ cup (125 mL) unsalted pistachios, crushed in a mortar and pestle

½ cup (125 mL) dry breadcrumbs

Salt

Pepper

1 cup (250 mL) goat cheese

Preheat the oven to 375°F (190°C).

For the first layer, place the zucchini slices in a baking dish just big enough to hold everything and brush with the pistachio pesto. Scatter the tomato and onion slices over the zucchini, followed by the pistachios and breadcrumbs.

For the second layer, place the zucchini in the opposite direction and repeat the process with the addition of dollops of ½ cup (125 mL) goat cheese. Season well with salt and pepper. Repeat until the zuc-chini is used up, then place the remaining ½ cup (125 mL) of goat cheese on top and garnish with the remaining pistachios.

Bake in the oven and until the zucchini is tender and the breadcrumbs are golden, approximately 20 to 30 minutes. Allow to rest and set before slicing.

PASTA SALAD *with* GREEN ONION DRESSING

Serves 4

OBEDIENT INGREDIENT Coconut

When do you like to serve a **pasta salad**? It's one of those dishes that works for everything: for a barbecue, for a picnic, packed in your lunch, as your lunch, as a side for dinner. It sits in the fridge nicely, it comes out cold and delicious and, if you want, you can heat it up. Pasta salad is the versatile pasta warrior. You can make a big batch and snack on it for a couple of days.

The **green onion dressing** is so nice you'll want to make it just in time and in just the right amount to maximize the flavour of the green onion. Buzz these ingredients in the blender and you're done. The **shredded coconut** adds a surprise texture.

The secret to a good pasta salad is tossing over the dressing while the pasta is still hot. This helps the flavour to penetrate while the pasta is cooling down. Don't eat it right away; let the flavours blend. This salad is a healthy alternative to traditional pasta salad as it doesn't contain any mayonnaise. The creaminess comes from the puréed herbs. You'll want all the textures and colours: the more festive the salad looks, the better it tastes.

Green Onion Dressing

½ cup (125 mL) olive oil
1 bunch green onions, white bottoms and
    green tops separated
1 small garlic clove, chopped
1½ Tbsp (22.5 mL) white wine vinegar
1 tsp (5 mL) Dijon mustard
2 Tbsp (30 mL) sour cream
Salt
Pepper

Heat the grill to medium-high heat.

Drizzle ½ tsp (2.5 mL) of the olive oil over the white bottoms of the green onion. Grill them until slightly softened and charred. Place the grilled green onion whites, green onion tops, garlic, white wine vinegar, Dijon mustard and remaining olive oil in a blender and purée until smooth. Transfer to a bowl, stir in the sour cream and season with salt and pepper.

Use all the green onion dressing for the pasta salad recipe.

Store in an airtight container refrigerated for up to three days.

Pasta Salad

¾ lb (375 g) bow tie pasta
1 Tbsp (15 mL) vegetable oil
1 red onion, cut into ¼-inch- (6 mm)
    thick rings
Salt
1 red bell pepper, diced
1 yellow bell pepper, diced
1 orange bell pepper, diced
Green Onion Dressing
1 cup (250 mL) chopped parsley
Pepper
1 cup (250 mL) shredded unsweetened
    coconut, toasted

Cook the pasta according to the package directions. Heat the grill to medium-high heat.

Place the cooked pasta in a large bowl and toss with 2 tsp (10 mL) of the vegetable oil.

Drizzle the remaining 1 tsp (5 mL) of vegetable oil over the red onion rings and season with salt. Grill the red onions until softened, approximately 10 minutes. Remove from the grill and roughly dice.

Add the peppers, red onion, green onion dressing, chopped parsley and salt and pepper to taste to the pasta. Mix to incorporate all the ingredients.

Garnish with toasted coconut.

I love soup. It's the perfect food. You start with the basics and add whatever you want—like you do with a sandwich, for example. I'd eat soup every day if my wife would let me get away with it, but she won't, so I don't. But I do go for lunch to a couple of soup spots I like.

Soup starts with water or stock; then you add meat, vegetables, legumes—whatever—let it boil, turn it down, let it sit, take it off the heat and enjoy. You can make a soup hearty by adding starch—rice, pasta, dumplings, or a lot of root veg—or you can keep it very light by using a light broth like a miso or strained vegetable broth.

Almost every culture has a tradition of bread and soup. In Mexico, shredded tortilla is added to soup. Bajans serve pumpkin soup with toasted croutons. In Vietnam they do the *banh mi*, served with their traditional *pho. Banh mi* is a baguette filled with chicken or sausage, with a sweet spicy mayo, a lot of big leafy herbs instead of lettuce and some julienned pickled carrots and sprouts.

Soup takes me back to my childhood. In the Caribbean I would feast on soups loaded with dumplings and ham and thickened with peas—very different from the chicken noodle soup I ate after coming home from playing hockey, after I'd moved to North America.

SOUP & SANDWICH

Celeriac

CELERIAC SOUP &
GORGONZOLA GARLIC BREAD

Serves 4

Celeriac is the root of the celery, the part in the ground. It ain't pretty but it has a very distinct celery-anise flavour.

The trick to a memorable soup is lots of flavour, which means lots of alliums—be they onions, leeks or shallots. This recipe takes a classic French-style soup with cream and wine and whatever produce is fresh and in season. You cook it down and purée it until smooth, the same way you'd make a cream carrot ginger soup. Here we use leeks, a classic ingredient in French soups as they offer a more refined flavour; they're smoother and not as sharp as onions.

The soup is inspired by the French classic vichyssoise, but instead of potato we're using celeriac. Peel off the outside skin and cook it like a potato. It's a super-easy vegetarian soup: cook, reduce and blend. Garnish with sour cream and black sesame seeds. For a very elegant soup, replace the celeriac with parsnip and add a bit of truffle oil.

In France, they'll often put a crouton, or a composed crouton with melted cheese, on top of soup. It's an idea that stems from French onion soup with bread and melted gruyère. This **gorgonzola garlic bread** is a simple version that contrasts the sharp flavour of the blue cheese against the sweet celeriac flavour of the soup for a truly monster flavour. And best of all, you can dip the bread in the soup. Come on, who doesn't love to dip?

A tip: don't cut the bread too thick. You want a little bit of chewiness from the bread but not too much. Cut it just thick enough for it not to become brittle, like a crostini, and to have just enough bite. Experiment and find the sweet spot.

Celeriac Soup

3 Tbsp (45 mL) butter

2 leeks, green top removed, roughly
   chopped

1 onion, roughly diced

3 sprigs thyme

2 bay leaves

½ cup (125 mL) dry white wine

1 celeriac, peeled, roughly diced

1 potato, peeled, roughly diced

6 cups (1.5 L) vegetable stock

1 cup (250 mL) 35% cream

Salt

Pepper

Pinch fresh nutmeg

¼ cup (60 mL) sour cream

1 Tbsp (15 mL) black sesame seeds for
   garnish

Place 2 Tbsp (30 mL) of the butter in a
pot over medium heat. Once the butter
has melted, place the leeks, onion, thyme
and bay leaves in the pot and stir until the
onion is translucent. Add the white wine
and simmer until the liquid is reduced by
two-thirds. Add the celeriac and potato
and stir. Add the vegetable stock and
bring to a boil, then reduce the heat to a
simmer.

   Cook, uncovered, until the celeriac is
tender, approximately 35 to 40 minutes.
Then transfer the whole mixture to a
blender and purée until smooth.

   Stir in the cream and the remaining
1 Tbsp (15 mL) of butter. Season the
celeriac soup with salt, pepper and
nutmeg.

   To serve, garnish with sour cream and
black sesame seeds.

Gorgonzola Garlic Bread

½ baguette, sliced

1 clove garlic, peeled

1 cup (250 mL) crumbled gorgonzola

Preheat the oven to 400°F (200°C). Line a
baking tray with parchment paper.

   Rub the baguette slices on one side
with the garlic clove. Crumble the gorgonzola overtop.

   Place the gorgonzola garlic bread on
the lined tray and place it in the oven until
the cheese has melted, approximately 2 to
5 minutes.

Duck

LENTIL SOUP *&* DUCK SANDWICH *with* MANGO CHUTNEY *&* SALTED PICKLED ONION

Serves 4

The inspiration for this tasty **lentil soup** was old-fashioned minestrone, with its hearty beans and vegetables. However, the taste and texture are quite different thanks to the lentils and the duck.

I grew up going to Edmonton's Chinatown every weekend with my father. We'd always stop to admire the **Peking duck** in the windows. Cooking a Peking duck is a very involved process. You need to blow the skin with an air pump, rest it, glaze it with hot honey water, then hang it overnight in the fridge to drain off all the excess water. The honey that remains on the duck sticks to the surface. The duck is cooked while hanging to help render the fat, and the honey gives a delicious sticky crispy exterior. To make things simple, I suggest you buy a cooked Peking duck, take it home and shred it.

Remove the skin, put it on a wire rack on top of a baking sheet and bake it slowly so it crisps up like bacon. Add this to the sandwich. Decadently delish.

If you can't get a Peking duck, get a duck breast. Roast it, crisp the skin and enjoy. If you do buy the Peking duck, shred the meat by pulling it off the bone. You need shredded pieces of duck to take full advantage of the tenderness of the meat.

The sandwich uses a fresh baguette with the inside scooped out so that the sandwich can hold more stuff and, when you bite into it, all the good stuff doesn't fly out onto your shirt. And it's not so bready. Store the scooped-out bread in the pantry for breadcrumbs for later. Since this sandwich is inspired by the Vietnamese *banh-mi* I use large leaves of fresh herbs instead of lettuce.

Duck lends itself to sweet things—think *duck à l'orange* or duck with plums—so **mango chutney** is an ideal condiment. Don't cook it too long, or it breaks up. You want little pieces of mango still intact so you get the texture with the taste.

The **pickled onion** recipe is so simple! And you can apply the process to cucumbers, green onions and carrots, all equally good in their own unique way. It's not a true pickle as there is no vinegar cure, so it should probably be called cured onion. Not to worry. It's still tasty.

With fatty foods, you need something acidic and sharp to cut the fat on your palate; the red wine vinegar and the salty red onions help to cut the fatness of the duck and balance the sweetness of the mango.

This is an easy meal to make on a school night. You pick up the duck, shred it, toss the bones in the broth and, while you make the rest of the meal, the broth is making itself.

Lentil Soup

1 store-bought cooked Peking duck, meat and bones separated

8 cups (2 L) chicken stock

1 Tbsp (15 mL) olive oil

½ red onion, diced

2 cloves garlic, chopped

2 celery stalks, finely diced

1 carrot, finely diced

2–3 bay leaves

½ cup (125 mL) red lentils, rinsed and drained

Salt

Pepper

3 plum tomatoes, seeded and diced

½ bunch chives, cut into ½-inch (1 cm) pieces

Shred the duck meat, keeping 1 cup (250 mL) for the soup and setting aside the remainder for the sandwich.

Place the chicken stock and the duck bones in a large pot and bring to a boil. Reduce the stock to a simmer, skim off any impurities and allow the stock to simmer for 30 minutes. Place the olive oil in a large pot over medium-high heat. Add the onion and the garlic and sauté until tender. Add the celery, carrot and bay leaves and sauté for approximately 2 minutes, just until the celery and carrot are slightly tender.

Strain the stock through a fine mesh strainer into another pot and bring to a boil. Add the lentils and reduce the heat to a simmer for 30 minutes. Season with salt and pepper and garnish with the 1 cup (250 mL) shredded duck meat, tomatoes and chives.

Mango Chutney

½ cup (125 mL) palm sugar, broken into pieces (or ¼ cup / 60 mL white sugar + ¼ cup / 60 mL brown sugar)

4 star anise, whole

1 cup (250 mL) water

Juice of 2 limes

2 ripe mangoes, peeled and diced

1 tsp (5 mL) chili flakes

Salt

"Everyone, and I do mean everyone, on the set of *Everyday Exotic* freaked out over this sandwich. I was a hero for the day when I made it. Our broadcaster wouldn't let us make duck on the show because duck was the dish of choice for every snooty chef on the channel looking to out-snoot the other snooty chefs. Duck was considered too fancy, not something anyone would make any day, let alone every day. It became my mission to get duck approved— I'm stubborn like that. As soon as the production executives tasted this sandwich they lifted the duck ban.

Duck Sandwich

1 baguette, cut in half lengthwise, inside of bread mostly removed

Shredded duck meat reserved from lentil soup recipe

Mango Chutney

Salted Pickled Onion

½ bunch chives, cut into ½-inch (1 cm) pieces

1 cup (250 mL) cilantro leaves

½ cup (125 mL) mint leaves

Salt

Pepper

Preheat the oven to 375°F (190°C).

Place the baguette and duck meat on a tray and heat them in the oven until the meat is warmed through and the baguette is lightly toasted. Remove the tray from the oven and place the baguette on a cutting board. Layer the shredded duck meat over one half of the baguette, followed by the mango chutney, salted pickled onion, chives, cilantro and then the mint.

Season the duck sandwich with salt and pepper, place the top of the baguette on the sandwich, cut into portions and serve.

Salted Pickled Onion

1 red onion, julienned

1 Tbsp (15 mL) salt

¼ cup (60 mL) red wine vinegar

Place the onion in a bowl, add the salt and toss. Let sit for 10 minutes. Rinse the salted onion under cold water, drain and place on a dry towel. Once the onion is dry, return it to the bowl and add the red wine vinegar. Toss to coat and pickle the onion.

Place the palm sugar and star anise with the water in a medium sauté pan over high heat and bring to a boil. Once the palm sugar has dissolved, add the lime juice. Continue to cook until the liquid has reduced to a thick, syrup-like consistency, approximately 5 minutes. Add the mangoes and chili flakes and season with salt. Cook for 5 to 7 minutes, stirring frequently, until the mango has become tender and the juices have reduced to a glaze.

Store in an airtight container for up to three days.

DAIKON SOUP *with* SHIITAKE CIGARS *&* STEAMED SWEET POTATO *with* GREEN ONION VINAIGRETTE

Serves 4

OBEDIENT INGREDIENT Daikon

Daikon doesn't often feature in a soup broth in North America, but it's a big player in this recipe, instead of carrots, onions, or celery, the more usual ingredients. Daikon is a long tubular root vegetable, used a lot in Japanese cuisine. It looks a lot like a turnip or radish. It's not as hot as a radish but still very flavourful. In this broth, it's not the key flavour, it's the flavour that ties everything else together. You need a very firm daikon for this recipe.

The **shiitake cigars** are wonton wrappers filled with a flavourful mushroom dice. Roll the wonton and seal it to create very tasty mushroom cigars. The cigars are blanched separately and added to the soup at the end so the starch doesn't cloud the broth.

You could also use this mushroom dice as a spread on a crostini or as the topping for a mushroom bruschetta.

Daikon Broth

¾ lb (375 g) daikon, peeled and chopped

One 6.3 oz (180 g) package enoki mushrooms, bottoms removed, tops reserved for garnish

½ lb (250 g) shiitake mushrooms (remove caps and reserve for shiitake cigars)

2 stalks celery, roughly chopped

1 large white onion, roughly chopped

1 large carrot, peeled and roughly chopped

1 red bell pepper, seeds removed and roughly chopped

½ bunch green onions, cut in half

3 bay leaves

1 Tbsp (15 mL) whole black peppercorns

1 bunch cilantro, reserve leaves for steamed sweet potato recipe

12 cups (2.8 L) cold water

Salt to taste

Place all of the ingredients in a large pot with the water, bring to a boil then reduce to a simmer for approximately 1 hour, uncovered. Strain the liquid through a fine mesh strainer into a clean pot, season with salt and keep hot.

Shiitake Cigars

1 Tbsp (15 mL) butter

1 Tbsp (15 mL) vegetable oil

3 cloves garlic, diced

2 shallots, diced

½ lb (250 g) shiitake mushroom caps, reserved from daikon broth recipe

Salt

Pepper

¼ cup (60 mL) Daikon Broth

1 Tbsp (15 mL) thyme, leaves picked

4 cups (1 L) water

¼ cup (60 mL) soy sauce

1 package wonton wraps

Eggwash made from 2 beaten eggs

Place the butter and the vegetable oil in a sauté pan over medium-high heat. Add the garlic and shallots and sauté until tender and translucent. Add the shiitake mushroom caps, season with salt and pepper and sauté until golden brown. Add the broth and thyme and stir. Allow the liquid to reduce until almost completely gone, remove the pan from the heat and place the mushroom mixture on a dish to cool.

Place the water with the soy sauce in a wide-mouthed sauté pan, bring to a boil, then reduce to a simmer.

Place a wonton wrapper on a clean, dry work surface and brush it with the egg wash. Spoon approximately 1 tsp (5 mL) of the mushroom mixture along the bottom of the wonton. Roll the wonton over tightly, ensuring that the mushroom mixture remains in the centre and the wonton is sealed. Press down on the edges, then cut them to trim any excess wonton. Place the shiitake cigars in the water-soy mixture until the wontons are cooked, approximately 5 minutes. Remove the shiitake cigars from the mixture and reserve for the daikon soup.

Daikon Soup

Daikon Broth

¼ cup (60 mL) soy sauce

3 Tbsp (45 mL) seasoned rice wine vinegar

1 Tbsp (15 mL) fish sauce

1 Tbsp (15 mL) honey

Shiitake Cigars

½ daikon, peeled and diced

Reserved enoki mushrooms tops from daikon broth recipe

½ bunch green onions, sliced thin

Chili oil as desired

Season the daikon broth with the soy sauce, rice wine vinegar, fish sauce and honey.

To serve, place five shiitake cigars in the bottom of a soup bowl. Pour daikon broth overtop and garnish the soup with the diced daikon, reserved enoki mushroom tops and green onion. Drizzle with chili oil.

Steamed Sweet Potato with Green Onion Vinaigrette

2 sweet potatoes, skins on, quartered and scored

¼ cup (60 mL) vegetable oil

3 cloves garlic, chopped

½ bunch green onions, chopped

3 Tbsp (45 mL) seasoned rice wine vinegar

1 Tbsp (15 mL) fish sauce

¼ tsp (1 mL) chili oil from chili paste

1 bunch cilantro leaves, reserved from daikon broth recipe

Steam the sweet potatoes until tender, approximately 20 minutes.

Meanwhile, heat the vegetable oil in a small sauté pan, add the garlic and lightly fry over medium heat until golden brown. Add the green onions, rice wine vinegar, fish sauce and chili oil, then combine well. Add the cilantro and toss to incorporate the flavours. Spoon the green onion vinaigrette over the steamed sweet potatoes.

> " In this recipe I substitute sweet potato as a starch instead of a sandwich. The broth is a very light clear broth that is full of flavour and restaurant worthy.

OBEDIENT INGREDIENT

Jerusalem Artichoke

JERUSALEM ARTICHOKE SOUP *with* BAGUETTE *with* THAI BASIL BUTTER

Serves 4

I f you've never tried a **Jerusalem artichoke**, put it on your bucket list. Immediately. It's one of life's great pleasures. Jerusalem artichokes, also called sunchokes, are oddly shaped little tubers with a distinctively sweet and earthy flavour. They have a very short growing season so snap 'em up when you can.

I like to drizzle this soup with a bit of olive oil and thyme. Fresh thyme and Jerusalem artichoke is one of those heavenly combinations that is simply too good to live without.

The baguette isn't strictly a sandwich, but once you've tasted the divine **Thai basil butter** you'll understand why it's in here. It's one of my favourite compound butter recipes. The butter is formed into a log so you can cut a sliver from the fridge to use anytime you want a bit of butter with a kick. It's a good way to add some flavour if you're sautéing eggs, or anything else you cook with butter. It also works as a condiment on the table.

Jerusalem Artichoke Soup

3 Tbsp (45 mL) olive oil
1 onion, diced
1½ lb (750 g) Jerusalem artichokes,
    roughly chopped
½ potato, quartered
3 sprigs thyme, tied with string,
    + 1 sprig, leaves picked for garnish
1 bay leaf
7 cups (1.75 L) water
½ cup (125 mL) 35% cream
Salt
Olive oil for drizzling

Heat 1 Tbsp (15 mL) of the olive oil in a
medium pot over medium heat. Add the
onion and sweat until tender and translucent. Add the Jerusalem artichokes and
potato and stir. Add the thyme, bay leaf
and water and continue to stir. Bring
to a boil, then reduce to a simmer. Once
the Jerusalem artichokes and the potatoes
are fork tender, remove the thyme and
bay leaf.

Transfer the soup to a blender and
purée in batches until smooth. Strain
the soup through a fine mesh sieve into a
clean pot, bring to a boil and then reduce
to a simmer for 1 minute. Add the cream
and season to taste with salt.

To serve, pour the soup into bowls
and garnish with a drizzle of olive oil and
thyme leaves.

Baguette with Thai Basil Butter

1 bunch Thai basil, washed, rinsed and
    leaves picked
1 cup (250 mL) butter, melted on low heat
    and cooled
½ baguette, toasted and cut into 4 pieces

Place the Thai basil leaves in a blender
and pour the melted butter over them.
Pulse the ingredients quickly until just
incorporated, being careful not to bruise
the Thai basil.

Transfer to a bowl and place it in the
freezer for 5 minutes. Remove the Thai
basil butter from the freezer and whisk
the mixture until well incorporated.
Return the Thai basil butter to the freezer
for another 5 minutes.

Remove from the freezer and spread
over the toasted baguette pieces.

**Serve the soup with a mountain of
baguette slices.**

Everyone loves a one-pot meal—by far the simplest way to cook a meal, it's also the simplest way to reduce the number of pots to wash.

My grandmother would always cook for us and it was often about "the pot." I'd go to the rice cooker to get the rice and then "the pot" to help myself to a delicious meal—sometimes it was chicken stew, sometimes *pelau* (a Trinidadian-style paella with meat instead of seafood) and *bun bun* (the crispy burned rice at the bottom of the pot)—scraping up all the tasty bits.

Stew is both a noun—for a bunch of great ingredients cooked and served from a single pot—and a verb—to cook with liquid. For a great one-pot meal, know what you're cooking and what the best pot is for cooking it. For example, I cook a braised pot roast in a tulip-shaped pot with enough room for everything to fit. I can cover it, leaving enough room for the steam to do its magic. For a gratin I use a shallow, wide-open ceramic baking dish, which exposes the most surface area available to melt the cheese.

What mistakes to do people make with one-pot meals? The most common one is to just turn the heat on high. One-pot is mostly about slower cooking at a lower temperature. Braising takes time. Give *pelau* a bit of time, or your whole dish will be *bun bun*.

Enjoy these one-pot meals with the same love with which they were shared.

ONE-POT MEALS

POTATO GUMBO

Serves 4

I love the deep, deep flavours of Cajun food. French cooking can have very subtle flavours, but Cajun just smacks you in the head and shouts in your face. Every now and again a smack in the head is a good thing. Cajun is pure and honest down-home cooking. I'm talking about hearty, flavourful food.

It's not only a versatile side dish, you can also serve it as a vegetarian main by leaving out the bacon and using vegetable stock instead of chicken. Fill up a bowl and eat it like a chili.

¼ cup (60 mL) + 1 Tbsp (15 mL)
   vegetable oil

1 medium white onion, diced

6 slices smoked bacon, large dice

2 cloves garlic, finely chopped

2 stalks celery, diced

1 bunch Swiss chard, roughly chopped,
   leaves and stems separated

1 large green bell pepper, diced

¼ cup (60 mL) all-purpose flour

2 bay leaves

2 cups (500 mL) water

2 cups (500 mL) chicken stock

Pinch cayenne

2 lb (1 kg) white potatoes, peeled
   and quartered

Salt

Pepper

Heat 1 Tbsp (15 mL) of the vegetable oil in a large high-sided sauté pan over medium heat. Add the onion and sauté until golden brown. Add the smoked bacon and garlic and continue to sauté until the bacon is crispy. Mix in the celery, Swiss chard stems and green pepper and continue to sauté until the vegetables are tender. Remove from the heat, place in a bowl and set aside.

Heat the remaining ¼ cup (60 mL) vegetable oil in the same sauté pan and then add the flour and the bay leaves. Stir with a wooden spoon, incorporating the flour and oil to form a paste, and cook until the flour becomes nutty brown in colour. Add the water, chicken stock and cayenne and stir.

Add the potatoes and reserved bacon mixture and cook over medium heat until the potatoes are tender and the liquid has reduced to give a thick consistency, approximately 30 minutes. Add the Swiss chard leaves and season with salt and pepper. Allow the potato gumbo to cook until the leaves are wilted.

OBEDIENT INGREDIENT

Okra

OKRA CHILI *with* CRISPY CORNMEAL OKRA & CHIPOTLE SOUR CREAM

Serves 4

At one time I tried to convince people that **okra** was not slimy and settled on calling it silky. But the truth is—okra is kinda slimy. My advice? Embrace the slime.

I love okra. The more you cook it, the "silkier" it gets, and in a chili, with all the chunks of meat and big veg, the smooth silkiness is kind of cool, especially with the crunchy exterior of the okra in the **crispy cornmeal okra** recipe. There's a dish in Trinidad called *callaloo* (also the name of a plant, in case you're interested), which is leafy greens with okra, cooked down and then buzzed in the food processor. You can spoon it over rice or eat it like a soup. It has a unique texture. If you want to make it and can't get fresh callaloo plant, use some baby spinach and okra.

Now let's talk about chili.

Chili really is the ultimate one-pot meal. I first encountered it in North America, because we don't make it in Trinidad. My sister started making it and I loved it. She was the one who got busy with the ground beef and tomatoes, introducing me to chili and lasagna.

Chili reheats beautifully, so make a nice big batch. Keep it handy to reheat. As a kid I used to go out and play road hockey until I was frozen, then I'd come in, heat up some leftover chili, get warmed up and fortified, and go back out.

To be assured of an awesome chili, cook the meat in the pan at high heat in small batches. If you crowd the meat you can't move it around and it starts to boil rather than brown. Remember, brown, don't boil. Pour off the fat. If you're on a low-fat diet you can drain the meat on a paper towel but the fat does add a rich flavour. When the meat is browned, remove it from the pan, then start sweating the onions and garlic. Add the meat back in, followed by the spices.

After you cook all the meat and onions, deglaze the bottom of the pan with a liquid to pull off all the flavour. In this recipe I use beer, which isn't uncommon to see in a chili because they just go so well together. The beer contributes to the cooking liquid. The alcohol boils off and the flavour remains.

The crispy cornmeal okra is like a nice bar snack. Take an okra finger, egg-wash it, roll it in cornmeal and deep-fry it. It will be almost raw, with a bright crunch from the cornmeal coating. And because it's cooked for such a short time, it's like a tempura vegetable—the slime doesn't have time to develop fully during cooking, if you're not one to "embrace the slime."

Dairy products like sour cream or yogurt calm the heat in a dish, but here, the **chipotle sour cream** adds flavour and heat. I like a spiced sour cream because it allows you to make a mild chili that everyone can enjoy and gives the fire-eaters a way to knock up the heat.

Chili Spice Mix

1 Tbsp (15 mL) garlic powder
1 Tbsp (15 mL) ground cumin seeds (use a mortar and pestle)
2 tsp (10 mL) hot or smoked paprika
1 tsp (5 mL) ground coriander seeds (use a mortar and pestle)
1 tsp (5 mL) chili flakes

Combine all the spices in a bowl.

Okra Chili

2 Tbsp (30 mL) vegetable oil
2½ lb (250 g) ground beef
1 bottle dark beer
1 sweet onion, diced
2 cloves garlic, chopped
1 red bell pepper, diced
1½ cups (375 mL) okra, sliced ½ inch (1 cm) thick
Chili Spice Mix
1–2 chipotle peppers, canned (depending on desired heat)
2 cups (500 mL) low-sodium beef stock
One 15 oz (400 mL) can diced tomatoes, with juice

1 can red kidney beans, drained and rinsed
¼ bunch cilantro, stems chopped, leaves picked
Salt
Pepper

Heat 1 Tbsp (15 mL) of the oil in a cast-iron pan over medium-high heat. Add the beef and cook until the moisture has evaporated and the beef is browned. Drain off any fat that has rendered and add the remaining vegetable oil with the onion, garlic, pepper and okra. Sauté over medium-high heat until lightly browned. Add the chili spice mix and chipotle pepper and stir. Deglaze with half of the bottle of beer, then add the browned beef and mix well. Add the stock and the diced tomatoes and bring to a boil. Cover the pot and reduce to a simmer.

After 1 hour, add the kidney beans and cilantro stems. Cook for half an hour over low heat, uncovered. Season with salt and pepper, remove from the heat and garnish with cilantro leaves.

Crispy Cornmeal Okra

4 cups (1 L) vegetable oil
½ cup (125 mL) cornmeal
¼ cup (60 mL) all-purpose flour
½ tsp (2.5 mL) black pepper
½ tsp (2.5 mL) sweet paprika
½ tsp (2.5 mL) garlic powder
2 egg whites
2 cups (500 mL) okra, washed and dried well, tip of stems and bottom ends removed
Salt

In a tall pot, heat the oil to 350°F (175°C). Line a baking tray with paper towel.

Combine the cornmeal, flour, black pepper, paprika and garlic powder in a bowl.

In a separate bowl, whisk the egg whites with a pinch of salt until frothy. Dip the okra in the egg whites, allowing any excess to drip off. Dip the okra in the flour mixture to coat and then carefully place in the hot oil.

Fry the okra until golden brown, approximately 3 minutes. Place on the prepared tray and season with salt. Repeat with the remaining okra.

Chipotle Sour Cream

1 cup (250 mL) sour cream (reduced fat if you prefer)
Juice of ½ lime
1 chipotle pepper, canned, finely chopped
Salt
Pepper

Combine all the ingredients in a bowl. Mix well to incorporate. Serve with cripsy cornmeal okra.

"Chili is the perfect meal for experimenting with spice mixes. Sure, you can go to the grocery store and buy taco mix, but all they've done is mix up a few different spices and put them in a package. And that's great if you don't have time. But my spice mix is fun and easy to make—cumin and chili (the key flavours of chili) with paprika, coriander and garlic powder. You can make up a batch and save the extra spice mix for a barbecue.

Plantain

TRINIDADIAN-STYLE CHICKEN *with* PLANTAIN GRATIN

Serves 4

The chicken method is a bit different in this recipe. Usually the chicken would be browned in oil. Here I'm adding sugar to make a caramel that adds flavour and browning to the meat.

You have to be careful not to burn the sugar or it will taste bitter. Watch over it so it continues to brown the meat. Don't fuss with it, though, just let it do its thing. You can add a bit less sugar if you want. Just scale it to your tastes and dietary needs.

Once the chicken is brown, just add the veg and let everything cook on the stove in the one pot. Simple and delicious.

Potato gratin is the starch gratin that we're most familiar with, but as plantain is the obedient ingredient here I have a **plantain gratin** instead. Plantain is a very firm banana

and a delicious starch alternative. It's very popular in the Caribbean, where it's called a "provision," just like cassava, breadfruit, potato or yam. Think of a root vegetable gratin as a plate of nachos; just replace the nachos with the plantain and add all the other ingredients as you would for a tray of killer nachos. The melted cheese and the pickled chilies really jump out from the mild sweet plantain

The **pickled topping** can also be used on nachos, instead of salsa. Add a bit of cheese, broil and watch the football game. You make the topping ahead and keep it in the fridge as a condiment, for a sandwich or for a pasta salad. It brings a beautiful spicy sweet flavour.

Ames's Marinade

½ cup (125 mL) vegetable oil
6 cloves garlic, chopped
2 shallots, roughly chopped
1 bunch green onion, chopped
1 bunch parsley leaves and stems,
    roughly chopped

Place all the ingredients in a blender
and purée. Transfer to a container and
refrigerate until needed.

Trinidadian-Style Chicken with Plantain

1 whole chicken, cut into pieces to match
    the size of a chicken thigh piece
Ames's Marinade
⅓ cup (80 mL) sugar
¼ cup (60 mL) vegetable oil
4 plum tomatoes, chopped
1 green chili, sliced in half, lengthwise
    (optional) (with or without seeds,
    depending on how hot you want it)
1 unripe plantain cut in half, lengthwise
    and chopped
½ white onion, finely diced
¼ cup (60 mL) Worcestershire sauce
½ cup (125 mL) chicken stock
Salt
1 cup (250 mL) cilantro, leaves picked

Marinate the chicken in half a batch
of Ames's marinade for a minimum of
45 minutes to a maximum of three days.

In a wide-based pan, heat the sugar
and vegetable oil over medium-high heat.
Swirl until the sugar caramelizes and
turns brown, approximately 7 to 10 minutes. As soon as the sugar caramelizes, add
the chicken, skin side down. Brown the
chicken on all sides, approximately
5 minutes. Add the tomatoes, chili, plantain, onion and Worcestershire sauce.
Stir. Add the chicken stock and bring to
a boil. Add the remaining half of Ames's

marinade and reduce to medium heat.
Cook for 30 to 40 minutes or until chicken
is fully cooked, season with salt and
remove from heat.

Garnish with cilantro before serving.

Pickled Topping

½ cup (125 mL) white wine vinegar
½ cinnamon stick
¼ cup (60 mL) water
2 jalapeños, seeded and sliced in
    ¼-inch (6 mm) pieces
1 shallot, sliced in ¼-inch (6 mm) pieces
1 Tbsp (15 mL) sugar
Salt

In a small pot, heat the white wine vinegar and cinnamon stick and water. Bring
to a boil. Add the jalapeños, shallot and
sugar, then mix well. Remove from the
heat. Season with salt, then let everything
sit in the vinegar for 10 minutes. Discard
the cinnamon stick and strain the liquid
through a fine mesh sieve, reserving only
the pickled shallot and jalapeños for the
plantain gratin. Discard the liquid.

*Store for up to three days refrigerated in
an airtight container.*

> "Ames's Marinade (my grandmother's marinade) is the secret ingredient in my Trini Chicken with Plantain. My grandmother got the name Ames because my sister couldn't say "Granny". The name stuck—by the time my grandmother passed, few people knew her birth name. Everyone called her Ames, and so her name lives on. Ames had a batch of her marinade in the fridge 365 days a year. She would put it in this stew, cook fish in it, use it on pork . . . you name it. I don't quite have it going all the time in my fridge, but I do love it. Ames would leave her meat and chicken in her marinade for up to three days and we would all chew the bones to get that last drop of flavour.

Plantain Gratin

4 ripe plantain, peeled
1 tsp (5 mL) vegetable oil
Salt
1 cup (250 mL) aged white cheddar, grated
3 green onions, chopped
Pickled Topping
¼ cup (60 mL) cilantro, leaves picked

Preheat the oven to broil.

Cut the plantain in half lengthwise.
Place the pieces in a baking dish, drizzle
with the vegetable oil and season with
salt. Broil for 5 to 7 minutes until slightly
caramelized.

Sprinkle the cheese and green onions
over the plantains and broil in the oven
for another 3 to 4 minutes until the cheese
is melted. Garnish with pickled topping
and cilantro.

These dishes are quick. And—easy!!!

Quiche is particularly quick and easy when you buy a premade shell—let me just get that in, before you email me about how a homemade crust is anything but easy. Barring the quiche crust, these dishes are aimed at getting on the table in much less than 30 minutes.

Everybody's life is so busy, whether you have no kids or four kids, one job or six jobs, so I won't take any more of your time—get cooking.

QUICK & EASY

BAKED EGGS

Serves 4

Baked eggs is a delicious "breakfast for dinner" meal, as well as a nice weekend breakfast. This method is easier than scrambling or anything else. Just crack the eggs into a little container, add whatever you like (cheese, asparagus, spam, anything), pop the dish in the oven and take it out a few minutes later for something that feels really special.

If you want to feed a family with this recipe, just use a bigger dish, so everyone can scoop out a piece. Cook it a bit longer to set the yolks completely, or pull it out a bit earlier if you like your eggs to run like fugitives. As versatile as a soup or a sandwich, baked eggs allow for dozens of combinations of ingredients and flavours. For a great anchor to the meal, add some pork belly (see recipe on page 163), bacon, pancetta, or even a few slices of a nice steak.

1 tsp (5 mL) vegetable oil

1 small shallot, thinly sliced

8 fresh eggs, room temperature

⅓ cup (80 mL) 35% cream

1 plum tomato, seeded and finely diced

1 Tbsp (15 mL) butter

Salt

Pepper

½ bunch chives, finely sliced

4 slices toast

Preheat the oven to 350°F (175°C).

Divide the vegetable oil and the shallot evenly among four ovenproof wide-mouthed ramekins.

Gently crack two eggs into each ramekin. Top the eggs evenly with cream, tomato and butter. Season with salt and pepper and bake for approximately 8 to 10 minutes until the egg whites have set.

Remove from the oven, garnish with chives and serve immediately with toast.

POTATO PANCAKES

Serves 4

These **potato pancakes** are a great starch component for a pork chop or roast chicken dinner. I like them because they're quick, hearty and substantial—potato with a bit of a crust is delicious. I serve three to a portion.

These potato pancakes work well with anything you would eat potato with at dinner time and they're great with breakfast if you have some leftover mashed potato. And they're so simple you can cook them at a campfire. If you want to impress someone, dress these up with a nice bit of lobster or crab—and you have a fresh elegant take on a main course. Or for a light lunch, add a bit of smoked salmon and a side salad of simple greens.

1 egg

1 cup (250 mL) 2% milk

½ cup (125 mL) all-purpose flour

2 tsp (10 mL) garlic powder

Salt

Pepper

5 loose cups (approx. 1.25 L) of chunky mashed potato (from 5 peeled potatoes, preferably Yukon gold)

1 bunch green onions, roughly chopped

1 Tbsp (15 mL) vegetable oil

1 Tbsp (15 mL) butter

Preheat the oven to 350°F (175°C).

In a bowl, beat the egg with ½ cup (125 mL) of the milk. Add the flour and mix well. Add the garlic powder. Season with salt and pepper to taste. Add the remaining ½ cup (125 mL) of milk and mix well.

Add the mashed potato and mix well. Add the green onions and incorporate.

Heat the vegetable oil in an ovenproof sauté pan over medium-high heat. Once the pan is hot, spoon the pancake mixture into the pan to form four pancakes. Add the butter to the pan. Flatten the pancakes for even cooking, cook for 4 minutes, then flip. Place the pan in the oven for 5 minutes until the potato pancakes are brown and cooked through.

OBEDIENT INGREDIENT

Prosciutto

GOAT CHEESE QUICHE *with* PROSCIUTTO *served with* GREEN BEAN SALAD *with* CRISPY PROSCIUTTO *&* WARM LEMON DRESSING

Serves 4

Quiche pastry is a basic pie shell. Bear in mind that with any baking like this, elevation and humidity will affect the liquid content slightly. If I'm making this recipe in the summer, or in the Caribbean, I add a little bit less water. How do you know when you have enough? Just as the dough is starting to clump together, stop adding water.

This recipe is a **goat cheese quiche**; if you don't have thyme in your pantry, stick with herbs that work well with the goat cheese—try tarragon or oregano.

If you buy a frozen pastry shell, you can save a lot of time, but making this dough is not difficult and you can always make it ahead of time.

Green bean salad joins this quiche as an accompaniment, which makes this an ideal vegetarian meal if you omit the prosciutto. The **prosciutto** pairs nicely with the asparagus, though, adding a lean salty pork flavour. Blanch the vegetables and crumble the crispy prosciutto on top like bacon bits.

My philosophy on quiche is: don't overcook it. You aren't making scrambled eggs in pastry. People tend to cook quiche until it is set firm and it just goes rubbery. You want it so that it sets but still has a little bit of a jiggle. I do like a little jiggle. The quiche should hold its form when you cut it, but still be very tender and light.

> "When my family moved to North America my mom really got busy learning other kinds of cooking and she was all over quiche. I ate a lot of quiche. A lot. Seriously. She used to make a great crab version. I still love a good quiche."

Pastry

2 cups (500 mL) all-purpose flour, sifted
½ lb (250 g) cold butter, cubed
½ tsp (2.5 mL) table salt
¼–½ cup (60–125 mL) ice water
1 egg beaten

In a large bowl, place the flour, butter and salt. Using the tips of your fingers, mix until the ingredients resemble coarse cornmeal. Add the iced water a little at a time until the dough just comes together. Remove the dough from the bowl, form into a disc, cover with plastic wrap and place it in the fridge for 1 hour (this can be done the night before).

Preheat the oven to 375°F (190°C).

Lightly flour your work surface, roll out the dough and place it in an 8-inch (20 cm) pan. (If you want to be able to remove the quiche easily, use a pan with a removable bottom.) Allow the dough to hang over the edges of the pan. Trim the edges slightly, still leaving an overhang of dough, and poke the pastry with a fork. Place the crust on a baking tray and cover the pastry with aluminum foil. Fill the pastry with dried beans or pastry weights and bake for approximately 15 minutes.

Remove the foil and beans and place the pastry back in the oven until the pastry is golden brown, approximately 10 minutes. Remove the pastry from the oven and, while it's still hot, brush a thin layer of the beaten egg overtop to seal the pastry.

Goat Cheese Quiche with Prosciutto

3 large shallots, cut in half, skins on
1 Tbsp (15 mL) olive oil
2 cups (500 mL) 2% milk
3 eggs, room temperature
4 sprigs thyme, leaves picked
¼ tsp (1 mL) salt
¼ tsp (1 mL) pepper
½ cup (125 mL) crumbled goat cheese
1 pastry crust
2 cups (500 mL) baby arugula
6 pieces of thinly sliced prosciutto

Preheat the oven to 375°F (190°C).

Place the shallots in a small ovenproof sauté pan, skin side up. Coat with olive oil, season with salt and roast for 30 minutes until tender. Remove the shallots from the oven and allow to cool.

Reduce the oven temperature to 325°F (160°C).

Peel the skins from the cooled shallots and set aside. Place the milk in a pot over low heat until scalded then set aside.

In a bowl, whisk the eggs, thyme, salt and pepper until incorporated. Slowly pour the warm milk into the egg mixture and continue whisking.

Scatter the roasted shallots and goat cheese into the pastry crust. Pour the egg mixture into the pastry crust. Place the quiche in the oven and bake for approximately 20 to 30 minutes, until the custard has set. Remove the quiche from the oven and allow it to cool.

Slice the quiche into portions and place the arugula and prosciutto overtop.

Crispy Prosciutto

8 pieces prosciutto, thinly sliced and cut into 1-inch (2.5 cm) pieces

Heat a non-stick sauté pan over medium-high heat. Place the pieces of prosciutto in the pan and cook until crisp. Remove the pan from the heat and reserve the prosciutto for the green bean salad.

Warm Lemon Dressing

3 Tbsp (45 mL) extra virgin olive oil
½ shallot, diced
Salt
¼ cup, skinless almonds, sliced
¼ cup (60 mL) sultana raisins
¼ cup (60 mL) raisins
¼ cup (60 mL) kalamata olives, pitted
Juice of 1 lemon
1 tsp (5 mL) honey
Pepper

Place 1 Tbsp (15 mL) of the olive oil in a pan over medium-high heat. Add the shallot, season with salt and sauté until tender. Add the almonds, sultanas, raisins and olives and mix to incorporate. Add the lemon juice and honey and stir. Add the remaining olive oil, season with salt and pepper and remove from the heat.

Green Bean Salad

1 bunch (¾ lb/375 g) asparagus, bottoms trimmed and blanched in salted water
½ lb (250 g) green beans, trimmed and blanched in salted water
Warm Lemon Dressing
Crispy Prosciutto

Cut the blanched asparagus and green beans into 1-inch (2.5 cm) pieces and place in a bowl. Pour the warm lemon dressing overtop, toss and garnish with the crispy prosciutto.

FAST-FRY STEAK *served with* SUNDRIED TOMATO *&* ROASTED RED PEPPER ORZO *&* MANGO CHOW

Serves 4

A **fast-fry steak** is a thin beef steak pounded with a mallet (or the meaty part of your hand) and cooked quickly in a cast-iron skillet. Dredge it in flour and fry it in butter and oil to add flavour and give it a nice crisp texture. The sage gives the butter a light herb flavour. You can transform this simple infused butter by swapping whichever herb you like best. For me, it depends on my mood and whatever is fresh. Or, let's face it, whatever is sitting in my fridge that day.

The **mango chow** is a take on a dish that I grew up eating in the Caribbean called chow, one of my all-time favourites. It's a great snack to tide kids, big and small, over between meals. It's also a great way to introduce hot spicy flavours to kids who may discover they really like it, like I do. Although it's normally made very very spicy, you can do it with oranges, mangos, apples, whatever fruit you prefer. It's nice as a snack and very nice as a fresh side dish.

In this recipe I use *sriracha*, which is a Vietnamese-style chilli paste, but feel free to use whichever type of hot sauce you have on hand or prefer. I have tried many different types and each one brings a unique flavour to the mango. Surprise yourself and feel free to experiment.

I love cooking with mango because it has such a refreshing flavour. Adding it to salads or sauces really brightens up the meal. It's impossible to feel sad when you're eating a

continued

mango and you'll be hard-pressed to find a person who doesn't love the taste. Most people tend not to cook with mango in their savoury dishes and it's a great surprise when its flavour comes through.

The **sundried tomato and roasted pepper orzo** is a very substantial starch dish, much like a pasta salad. Because the starch is the little rice-shaped orzo, all the pieces in the salad are chopped very small so all the flavours can sit on your fork at the same time. If the sundried tomato is too big it will push the orzo off the fork: you'll end up with sundried tomato all by itself and no orzo. And that's no fun at all.

Make the dressing before you finish boiling the orzo because you'll want to dress the hot pasta right away. Orzo is a small pasta so it loses heat quickly. The hot pasta sucks up the flavour of the dressing as it cools as well as helping to keep each grain of orzo separate.

Mango Chow

1 unripened mango, peeled and cut
    into strips
Juice of 1 lemon
1 tsp (5 mL) *sriracha*, or hot sauce
Pinch sugar
Salt
Pepper

Place all the ingredients except salt and pepper in a bowl and toss to combine. Allow the mango salad to marinate for half an hour and up to one hour. Season to taste with salt and pepper just before serving.

Serve the mango chow as an accompaniment to the meal or as a snack.

Sundried Tomato and Roasted Red Pepper Orzo

1 cup (250 mL) orzo
1 cup (250 mL) diced roasted red bell
    peppers
1 cup (250 mL) sundried tomatoes packed
    in oil, diced
Zest of 1 lemon
1 clove garlic, puréed
Salt
Pepper
½ bunch parsley, chopped

Cook the orzo according to the package directions, then transfer while warm to a bowl.

Add the roasted red peppers, sundried tomatoes, lemon zest and garlic and toss. Season with salt and pepper, add the chopped parsley and toss to incorporate before serving.

Fast-Fry Steak

Four ½ lb (250 g) fast-fry steaks, flattened
    with a mallet
Salt
Pepper
¼ cup (60 mL) all-purpose flour
½ bunch sage, leaves picked
2 Tbsp (30 mL) butter
1 Tbsp (15 mL) vegetable oil

Heat a cast-iron pan over high heat.

Season the steaks with salt and pepper. Place the flour on a plate and dredge the steaks in it.

Place the sage, butter and oil in the hot cast-iron pan. Place the steaks in the pan and sear for 30 seconds on each side. Remove from the heat.

Persimmon

PORK LOIN CUTLET *with* SAUTÉED PERSIMMONS *served with* BARLEY RISOTTO *&* PERSIMMONS *with* MINTED BROWN SUGAR

Serves 4

The **persimmon** and **chili** are sautéed in the same way as broccoli and garlic. Inspired by the tried and true "apples and pork," the persimmon is reminiscent of apples but the texture is crunchy, tender and substantial. Its fruit flavour goes so well with the sweetness of the **pork** and the mild heat of the chilies. And it works well with the floral flavour of the rosemary. **Rosemary** is a strong flavour that is best used sparingly, so be careful.

I like to serve this dish as a nest of **barley risotto** with the pork cutlet on top and the persimmon blessing the top of the cutlet.

> "You may be asking yourself, "Why did they put a risotto into a chapter called Quick and Easy?" The answer: To dispel the myths about risotto being difficult. This risotto uses barley. The trick is to let it cook gently so it releases the gluten slowly for the creamy consistency. It's not difficult or challenging, but you can't walk away from it and do something else. Risotto demands your full attention. But it is so worth the effort.

Pork Loin Cutlet

1 cup (250 mL) all-purpose flour

2 Tbsp (30 mL) vegetable oil

½ lb (250 g) pork loin, sliced into ¼-inch (6 mm) thick cutlets and pounded between plastic wrap

1 Tbsp (15 mL) fennel seed, toasted and ground in a mortar and pestle

Salt

Pepper

2 Tbsp (30 mL) butter

Place the flour on a large plate. Heat the vegetable oil in a sauté pan over medium-high heat and season the pork with the ground fennel seeds and salt and pepper to taste. Coat the cutlets with flour, place two in the pan (or as many that can fit without crowding the pan) and add the butter. Once the cutlets are golden brown on one side, approximately 2 minutes, turn them over, sear on the other side, then remove from the heat. Repeat with the remaining cutlets and set aside until assembly. To keep warm, place the cooked meat on a warm plate tented with aluminum foil.

Sautéed Persimmons

1 Tbsp (15 mL) butter

1 sprig of rosemary

2 firm persimmons, tops removed and sliced into ¼-inch (6 mm) thick wedges

1 red finger chili, sliced thinly on a bias

½ tsp (2.5 mL) sesame oil

Salt

Pepper

Heat the butter and rosemary in a sauté pan over medium heat. Once the butter has melted, place the persimmons in the pan and sauté until golden brown. Add the chili and sesame oil and season with salt and pepper. Toss to combine the ingredients, then remove the pan from the heat and set aside until assembly.

Barley Risotto

1 Tbsp (15 mL) olive oil

1 bunch green onions, whites minced, greens thinly sliced and reserved for garnish

1½ cups (375 mL) pearl barley

1 bay leaf

½ cup (125 mL) dry white wine

5 cups (1.25 L) hot chicken stock

3 Tbsp (45 mL) soy sauce

½ cup (125 mL) grated Parmesan

1 Tbsp (15 mL) lemon zest, finely chopped

Salt

Pepper

Heat the olive oil in a large, high-sided sauté pan over medium heat. Add the green onion whites and cook until tender and translucent. Add the barley and bay leaf and stir to coat with the oil. Add the white wine, allow it to reduce until almost gone, then add half the chicken stock with the soy sauce and stir. Once the barley has absorbed the liquid, add the remaining stock and stir. Once the liquid is absorbed and the barley is creamy and thick in texture, approximately 20 minutes, remove it from heat. Add the Parmesan and lemon zest, season with salt and pepper, stir and set aside.

Garnish with the green onion slices before serving.

Persimmons with Minted Brown Sugar

4 ripe persimmons, tops removed, peeled and diced

¼ cup (60 mL) brown sugar

¼ cup (60 mL) hand-torn mint

1 Tbsp (15 mL) lime zest

Pinch salt

Place the diced persimmons in a bowl. Add the remaining ingredients, toss and serve.

Spoon the barley risotto in the centre of a serving plate. Place one large or two smaller pieces of the pork loin cutlet over the barley risotto. Spoon the sautéed persimmons overtop the pork loin cutlet and enjoy.

Chipotle

CHIPOTLE CHICKEN QUESADILLAS *with*
SMASHED WHITE BEANS *&* CORN SALSA *&*
TOMATO WATERMELON SALSA

Serves 4

Chipotle comes from the smoked jalapeño pepper and has become popular in North America over the last few years because of its strong smoky flavour. Warning: a little goes a long way; too much will have you tasting chipotle in your dreams. Start off with just a pinch and add more as you cook until you find the level you like.

Smashed white beans is my take on a hummus, with white bean and sage. It's a good meatless filling for the quesadilla.

The **corn salsa** is simply a condiment to serve with the quesadilla, the same way you'd serve a tomato salsa.

The **tomato watermelon salsa** tricks the mind because you don't really notice the watermelon, and its fresh flavour surprises you when you're expecting only tomato. Watermelon and savoury flavours naturally work together.

I love **cilantro**. People will often throw out the stems and the little white root, but so much of the flavour lives in these parts and it adds a real punch to the salsa. Wash the root thoroughly to get rid of the trapped dirt; keep going until it is dirt free and nearly white. Chop it up and keep it and the stems.

> "The heart of this dish is meat or poultry and cheese. I've made it with leftover duck and brie, and turkey and mozzarella.
> Make sure you put cheese all the way to the edges and press it down with your hand so the melted cheese will hold it all together. Cook it medium or medium-low so everything cooks and binds together. Slowly crisp up the bottom and warm everything through.

Chipotle Chicken

1 Tbsp (15 mL) vegetable oil
1 onion, diced
3 cloves garlic, chopped
2 chipotle peppers in canned adobo sauce, chopped
¼ cup (60 mL) apple cider vinegar
2 Tbsp (30 mL) adobo sauce
2 Tbsp (30 mL) molasses
1 tsp (5 mL) coriander seeds, ground
3 cups (750 mL) shredded chicken (left over from roasted chicken)
5 sprigs thyme, tied with string
Salt
Pepper

Heat the vegetable oil in a large cast-iron pan over medium heat. Add the onion and sauté. Once golden brown, add the garlic and stir. Add the chipotle peppers, apple cider vinegar, adobo sauce, molasses and ground coriander and stir until incorporated. Add the shredded chicken and thyme to the mixture and stir. Season with salt and pepper, remove the pan from heat and set aside.

Smashed White Beans

2 Tbsp (30 mL) olive oil
½ onion, diced
2 cloves garlic, chopped
1 Tbsp (15 mL) roughly chopped fresh sage
One 12 oz (340 g) can white beans, rinsed and drained
½ tsp (2.5 mL) chipotle chili powder
Salt
Pepper

Heat the olive oil in a sauté pan over medium heat, add the onion and garlic and cook until tender and translucent. Add the sage, stir to incorporate then add the white beans. Cook together until the beans are warmed; remove from the heat and smash with a potato masher or fork.

Season with chipotle chili powder, salt and pepper and set aside.

Corn Salsa

3 cobs of corn, husked
1 small red bell pepper, seeded and diced
1 jalapeño, seeded and diced
½ English cucumber, seeded and diced
¼ medium red onion, diced
¼ bunch cilantro, stems finely chopped, leaves roughly chopped
1 tsp (5 mL) olive oil
Salt
Pepper
Preheat the grill. Place the cobs of corn on the grill and cook for approximately 8 to 10 minutes until the corn is tender and charred. Cut the kernels off the cobs of corn and place them in a bowl. Add the remaining ingredients, except salt and pepper, and toss. Season to taste with salt and pepper and set aside.

Store in an airtight container for up to three days.

Tomato Watermelon Salsa

4 plum tomatoes, seeds removed and diced
2 green onions, finely sliced
1 cup (250 mL) seedless watermelon, diced
Zest and juice of 1 lime
2 Tbsp (30 mL) cilantro stems and leaves, chopped
Salt
Pepper

Place all the ingredients, except salt and pepper, in a bowl. Toss, season with salt and pepper and set aside.

Store in an airtight container for up to 24 hours.

Assembly

1 Tbsp (15 mL) olive oil
Smashed White Beans
Chipotle Chicken
One 8–10 oz (230–300 g) wheel of Brie, cut into long pieces
2 cups (500 mL) shredded aged white cheddar
1 cup (250 mL) crumbled blue cheese
1 package soft tortilla shells

Heat the olive oil in a cast-iron pan or a large sauté pan over medium heat. To assemble the quesadillas, place the desired combinations of smashed white beans, chicken and cheeses on half of a tortilla.

Fold the tortilla over and place it in the hot pan. Flip the tortilla once it is crispy and golden and repeat with the other side.

Remove the tortilla from the pan and serve with the tomato watermelon salsa and corn salsa.

Water Chestnut

SHRIMP *&* PORK TACOS *with* TOMATO SALSA *&* CREAMED AVOCADO *&* ENDIVE WATER CHESTNUT SALAD

Serves 4

The **water chestnut** is a nice crunchy vegetable with the texture of a crisp apple. It keeps its integrity and its crunch as it cooks. Its flavour is a mild honey sweetness, almost neutral, so it's the perfect way to add texture to a dish without upsetting the flavours. In this case, it's the perfect texture to add to the soft bounce of the **pork** and **shrimp**. And it hosts the flavours of the **taco** mix impeccably.

The **creamed avocado** is basically a guacamole cut with sour cream and lime for extra creaminess.

The **endive water chestnut salad** is all assembly once you've glazed the **walnuts** with the honey.

Shrimp and Pork Filling

1 tsp (5 mL) vegetable oil
¾ lb (375 g) ground pork
1 shallot, diced
1 clove garlic, diced
1 green chili, chopped
2 Tbsp (30 mL) ground cumin
2 tsp (10 mL) smoked paprika
15 large shrimp, shelled, deveined
   and roughly chopped
½ cup (125 mL) canned water chestnuts,
   rinsed, drained and diced
2 Tbsp (30 mL) chopped cilantro stems
Zest and juice of 1 lime
Pinch sugar
Salt

In a cast-iron pan, heat the vegetable oil over medium heat. Place pork in the pan and sauté until brown and caramelized. Once pork has browned, add shallot, garlic and chili and cook for 1 to 2 minutes.

Add the cumin and smoked paprika and stir. Then add the shrimp and stir. Once the shrimp have turned pink, add the water chestnuts and stir. Add the cilantro stems, lime zest and juice and sugar. Season with salt to taste. Stir, remove the pan from the heat and set aside for the taco assembly.

Tomato Salsa

3 plum tomatoes, diced
2 green onions, chopped
Juice of ½ lime
¼ bunch cilantro, stems chopped,
   leaves picked
Pinch sugar
Salt

Place the tomatoes and green onions in a small bowl. Add the lime juice and cilantro stems and leaves. Mix together and season with sugar and salt. Set aside for the taco assembly.

Store in an airtight container refrigerated for up to three days.

Creamed Avocado

2 avocados, roughly chopped
Juice of 2½ limes
¼ bunch green onions, chopped
¼ cup (60 mL) sour cream (reduced fat if
   you prefer)
2 Tbsp (30 mL) sugar
Salt

Place the avocados in a bowl with the lime juice and chopped green onions. Add the sour cream and sugar. Mash until the mixture is incorporated and season with salt. Set aside for the taco assembly.

Store in an airtight container refrigerated for up to three days

Honey Glazed Walnuts

1 cup (250 mL) walnuts
2 Tbsp (30 mL) honey
Pinch cayenne
Pinch salt

Preheat the oven to 350°F (175°C). Line a baking tray with parchment paper.

Place the walnuts on the baking tray. Drizzle the honey over walnuts and season with cayenne and salt. Place the tray in the oven and bake until the walnuts are golden brown, approximately 10 minutes.

Endive and Water Chestnut Salad

2 endives, leaves separated
2 cups (500 mL) canned water chestnut
   halves, rinsed and drained
1 red finger chili, sliced
1 Tbsp (15 mL) honey
1 Tbsp (15 mL) white wine vinegar
Juice of 1 lime
Salt
Honey Glazed Walnuts

" There are two parts to this dish: the taco and the salad.
The taco uses my homemade taco mix which is added to chopped fresh chili and diced garlic. Delicious. Add the spices and onions to the browned meat, stir in clean, chopped shrimp for 30 seconds, then drop this into your taco shell, dress it your way and enjoy.

Place the endives, water chestnuts and sliced chili in a bowl. Add the honey, white wine vinegar and lime juice and gently toss. Season with salt and garnish with honey glazed walnuts.

Assembly

8 soft tortilla shells, warmed over grill or
   in microwave for 30 seconds
Shrimp and Pork Filling
Creamed Avocado
Tomato Salsa
Cilantro stems with leaves, for garnish

Place a tortilla shell on a plate. Spoon shrimp and pork filling into the centre of the taco.

Spoon creamed avocado and tomato salsa overtop. Garnish the taco with cilantro and serve with the endive and water chestnut salad.

I like to go on about being improvisational and spontaneous—and I am. But the chef in me needs things to be meticulously organized. Luckily my executive producer Al Magee brings order to my chaos. When we found ourselves with all these great recipes that defied classification and were falling out of the chapter headings we started to panic—we couldn't make a "nuts" chapter and just have one recipe! So under the heading of Bonus Bites, here are some of my favourites of those great recipes, with some added love for an everyday meal.

Enjoy these recipes and serve them with as much love as they were created with.

BONUS BITES

HUMMUS

Serves 4

OBEDIENT INGREDIENT Chickpeas

Another shoutout to my Greek peeps, but this recipe is one I make for my kids. It takes all of three minutes to make this in the food processor from canned **chickpeas**. It's so flavourful I make it in batches and it lasts in the fridge all week long. I start to think about digging into the hummus dip on the drive home and when I get in, it's the first thing I'll eat. You can switch out the chickpeas for white navy beans and add a bit of sage for another robust dip with a very different flavour. It kills on a dip platter!

One 19 oz (540 mL) can of chickpeas, rinsed and drained

2 Tbsp (30 mL) plain yogurt (reduced fat if you prefer)

Juice of 1 lemon

1 clove garlic

½ cup (125 mL) + 1 Tbsp (15 mL) extra virgin olive oil

1 red bell pepper, diced

Pinch sugar

Salt

1 bunch parsley, chopped

Pinch of sweet paprika

Place the chickpeas, yogurt, lemon juice and garlic in a blender. As the ingredients are processing, pour in ½ cup (125 mL) of the olive oil in a slow, steady stream.

Transfer the mixture to a bowl and set aside.

In another small bowl, place the red pepper, sugar and salt to taste. Mix to incorporate, then add the parsley and mix again.

Sprinkle the paprika over the hummus dip and top with the red pepper and parsley topping.

Drizzle the remaining 1 Tbsp (15 mL) of olive oil around the hummus.

PEAR CHUTNEY

Serves 4

OBEDIENT INGREDIENT Cardamom

This **pear chutney** is a good recipe for teaching yourself how to make chutney. Once you've mastered pear you can swap it out for persimmon, cherries, mango and blends to make different kinds of chutney. The secret to any good chutney is to keep some texture and bite to the fruit or it breaks down and turns into a compote.

1½ Tbsp (22.5 mL) butter
1 shallot, minced
3 bosc pears, peeled, cut in large dice
⅓ cup (80 mL) sugar
1 Tbsp (15 mL) white wine vinegar
1 green chili, sliced
1 Tbsp (15 mL) minced ginger
½ stick cinnamon
½ tsp (2.5 mL) ground cardamom

Heat 1 Tbsp (15 mL) of butter in a sauté pan over a medium-low temperature. Add the shallot and cook until translucent. Add the pears, stir and cook until the pears are tender.

Add the sugar and stir until it dissolves. Add the vinegar and stir again. Mix in the chili, ginger, cinnamon and cardamom and stir, incorporating all the flavours.

Cook the pear chutney until the liquid has evaporated, approximately 4 minutes, then remove it from the heat and add the remaining butter and stir.

SPICED CASHEW NUTS

Serves 4

OBEDIENT INGREDIENT Cashew Nuts

Heed this warning. Make these **spiced cashew nuts** once and you'll be hooked and looking to invent ways to serve them. You can serve them as an element inside a salad or as a bar snack for watching the game, sneak them into the kids' lunch, or pack them in your knapsack for a hike. This recipe works for many other nuts (I think I'd only advise against using macadamias) but the cashews are my favourite.

1 tsp (5 mL) butter
½ cup (125 mL) unsalted cashews
Pinch of hot or smoked paprika
Pinch of salt

In a small sauté pan, melt the butter over medium heat. Add the cashew nuts and toss until golden brown. Remove the pan from the heat then add the paprika and salt. I challenge you to just have one.

TOASTED SOY NUTS MIX

Serves 4

OBEDIENT INGREDIENT Soy Nuts

This mix is a great bar snack to serve before dinner and a nice topping for a casserole or anything else you might want a crunchy topping on. Now, this is snack food at its best.

½ cup (125 mL) vegetable oil
1 shallot, diced
3 cloves garlic, diced
½ Tbsp (7.5 mL) diced ginger
1 cup (250 mL) slightly ground roasted soy nuts (use a mortar and pestle)
Salt

In a sauté pan, heat the vegetable oil over medium heat. Add the shallot and stir constantly until lightly browned. Add the garlic and ginger and continue stirring until lightly browned. Do not allow them to burn. Add the soy nuts and lightly toast for 1 to 2 minutes. Remove the pan from the heat and season the mixture with salt.

GINGER BUTTER POTATOES

Serves 4

OBEDIENT INGREDIENT Ginger

Potatoes often get the least consideration when it comes to experimentation. They are so commonplace: the reason exactly I felt it was necessary to give them a little bit of gingerly love.

2 Tbsp (30 mL) ginger butter from
 Ginger Butter Log (page 71)
2 lb (1 kg) new potatoes, boiled in
 salted water and cut in half
Salt

Place the ginger butter in a sauté pan over low heat. Once it has melted, add the potatoes to the pan. Toss until the potatoes are warmed and coated with the ginger butter, approximately 5 minutes. Remove from the heat and season with salt.

CURRIED CHICKPEA SALAD

Serves 4

OBEDIENT INGREDIENT Curry Powder

A **chickpea salad** can serve as both the protein and the starch of a meal. I love this salad as a bean salad for a family-style dinner party. I spike up the flavour with a touch of toasted **curry powder,** just to make an everyday bean salad taste like it has a story to tell.

1 tsp (5 mL) vegetable oil

½ onion, finely diced

1 carrot, finely diced

1 clove garlic, finely diced

2 Tbsp (30 mL) curry powder

Splash dry white wine

One 19 oz (540 mL) can chickpeas, rinsed and drained

4 plum tomatoes, roughly chopped and seeds removed

1 cup (250 mL) chicken stock

1 Tbsp (15 mL) sugar

Salt to taste

1 Tbsp (15 mL) butter, cold

In a sauté pan, heat the vegetable oil over medium heat and sweat the onion. Add the carrot and garlic and stir. Once the garlic has browned slightly, add the curry powder and stir well.

Add a splash of white wine and stir to deglaze the pan. Add the chickpeas and tomatoes and stir again. Pour in the chicken stock, cover the sauté pan with a lid and simmer for 10 minutes. Season the curried chickpeas with the sugar and salt. Remove the sauté pan from the heat and add the cold butter to finish.

ARUGULA SALAD

Serves 4

OBEDIENT INGREDIENT Arugula

A simple assembled salad: slice some figs, dress some arugula and toss in some torn buffalo mozzarella. It's easy and has a whole lot of flavour. Maybe it's the peppery taste of the **arugula**, but this salad is a great example of a dish that does not have to be complicated to taste fantastic. It's all about the fresh taste of the freshest ingredients combining to create something that seems extraordinary.

2 Tbsp (30 mL) olive oil

2 tsp (10 mL) red wine vinegar

Salt

6 buffalo mozzarella bocconcini balls, torn in half

4 figs, quartered

6 cups (1.5 L) baby arugula

Mix the olive oil and red wine vinegar together, season with salt and set aside.

Place the buffalo mozzarella bocconcini round the edge of a plate. Arrange the figs in between the pieces of mozzarella. Pile the arugula in the centre of the plate and drizzle the dressing over the entire salad.

LYCHEE CUCUMBER SALAD

Serves 4

OBEDIENT INGREDIENT Lychee

If you use canned **lychee**, this is really easy, but there is nothing quite like a fresh lychee if you can find them during their short season. Dump and drain the lychee, chop some **cucumber**, whisk up the very simple dressing and you have a fresh *à la minute* salad. Cucumber salad should be dressed just as you're serving it to prevent the cucumber from wilting with the acids in the dressing.

1 English cucumber

1 cup (250 mL) lychees, peeled, pitted and halved

3 stems cilantro, finely chopped and leaves picked (reserved for garnish)

2 red Thai chilies, pith and seeds removed and finely diced

Zest and juice of 2 limes

1 Tbsp (15 mL) seasoned rice wine vinegar

1 tsp (5 mL) sugar

Salt

Cut the cucumber in half lengthwise and scrape out the seeds with a spoon. Then quarter the cucumber and cut into ¼-inch- (6 mm) thick dice.

In a bowl, mix together the cucumber, lychees, cilantro stems and chilies. Add the lime zest and juice, rice wine vinegar, sugar and salt to taste and toss well to coat the vegetables.

Before serving, garnish with the reserved cilantro leaves.

CUCUMBER FETA SALAD

Serves 4

OBEDIENT INGREDIENT Feta

This one is for all of my Greek friends out there who are sick
of getting bad Greek salads at dinner parties or restaurants.
Here is a simple respectable recipe for a classic.

1 medium English cucumber, deseeded
   and sliced

1½ cups (375 mL) feta cheese, crumbled

¼ cup (60 mL) kalamata olives

½ lemon

3 Tbsp (45 mL) extra virgin olive oil

¼ cup (60 mL) mint leaves, torn

1 Tbsp (15 mL) dried oregano

Salt

Pepper

Place the sliced cucumber on a plate and
crumble the feta overtop. Add the kalamata olives, juice the lemon over the salad
and drizzle with the olive oil.

Garnish with the torn mint leaves and
season with oregano and salt and pepper
to taste.

CHINESE ROAST PORK

Serves 4

OBEDIENT INGREDIENT Hoisin Sauce

This dish is all about the sauce, and the sauce is all about making the exterior of the **pork tenderloin** all sticky and sweet and delicious. It's an easy sauce and an easy dish for a backyard patio party.

Confession time: this is a quickie version of the Chinese barbecued pork you see hanging in the windows in Chinatown.

MARINADE

3-inch (8 cm) piece of ginger

6 cloves garlic

1 shallot

½ cup (125 mL) oyster sauce

¼ cup (60 mL) hoisin sauce

2 Tbsp (30 mL) tomato paste

Place the ginger, garlic and shallot in a blender and purée. Transfer the mixture to a bowl and add the oyster sauce, hoisin sauce and tomato paste. Stir to incorporate.

ROAST PORK

2 pork tenderloins (approximate total weight of 10 oz/300 g), silverskin removed

Oyster Sauce Marinade

1 Tbsp (15 mL) vegetable oil

Place the pork tenderloins in a baking dish with half the oyster sauce marinade. Turn them to ensure that they are completely covered with marinade and place the dish in the fridge to marinate for a minimum of half an hour to a maximum

of overnight.

Preheat the oven to 400°F (200°C).

Heat the vegetable oil in a large, oven-proof sauté pan over medium-high heat. Remove the pork tenderloins from the fridge and place them in the sauté pan, searing the tenderloins on all sides.

Baste the pork with the remaining oyster sauce marinade and transfer the sauté pan to the oven until the pork is cooked through, approximately 20 minutes.

Allow the pork to rest for 15 minutes before serving.

CRISPY GLAZED PORK BELLY

Serves 4

OBEDIENT INGREDIENT Pork Belly

Pork belly is the same cut used for bacon and Italian pancetta. China has a mouth-watering dish of glazed pork belly cubes called Mao's Pork Belly, served at what was Chairman Mao's favourite restaurant. Pork belly is not something you want to eat all the time, unless you love your doctor, but it's a nice little treat to have under your belt. It's also very, very, very, very tasty. Stupid tasty. Crazy tasty. You can serve it as the main protein in a menu—if you can get it to the plate without eating it all first. A very versatile, very tasty piece of meat.

1½ cups (375 mL) cider vinegar
1 cup (250 mL) brown sugar
5 cloves
3 bay leaves
1 Tbsp (15 mL) salt
1 tsp (5 mL) whole black peppercorns
1½ lb (750 g) pork belly, cut into 1-inch (2.5 cm) cubes

Make a pickling liquid first, by placing all the ingredients, except the pork belly, in a pot. Bring to a boil, then reduce to a simmer.

Place the pork belly in a pot of cold, salted water and bring to a boil. Once the water comes to a boil, skim it to remove the impurities. Reduce the temperature to a simmer for approximately 10 minutes.

Strain the pork belly from the salted water and rinse. Place the pork belly pieces into the pickling liquid and simmer for approximately 30 to 45 minutes, until tender.

Preheat the oven to 400°F (200°C). Remove the pork belly from the pick-

ling liquid and pat dry. In a large cast-iron pan over medium heat, sear the pork belly, season with salt and pepper and place it in the oven.

Check on the pork belly constantly, turning the pieces over to ensure that all the sides are crispy, approximately 5 minutes, then remove it from the oven.

Strain 2 cups (500 mL) of the pickling liquid into a small pan through a fine mesh sieve and reduce it by two-thirds until the liquid achieves a thick-syrup consistency.

Place the reduced pickling liquid, now a glaze, in a bowl with the crispy pork belly and toss to coat.

There are few chefs who do both savoury and pastry. I'm not a pastry chef. It requires a whole different mindset. It's almost like being a scientist because you follow the detailed instructions of the recipe to the gram. Cooking leaves room for improvisation and a real margin for error. There is flexibility and forgiveness. I like flexibility and forgiveness.

Desserts just aren't that flexible and they can be very unforgiving.

Maybe the real truth is that I just don't have the patience to measure precisely and do the same things over and over again. I like to play and I like to invent. My wife does all the baking at home.

DESSERTS

VANILLA SOY MILKSHAKE

Serves 4

This **vanilla soy milkshake** is old school, inspired by the malt shop counter. It's just soy milk and good quality vanilla ice cream. Change the flavour of the ice cream and you have a brand new dessert.

4 cups (1 L) vanilla bean ice cream
3 cups (750 mL) soy milk

Place the ice cream and milk in a blender and mix until smooth. Then divide between four glasses.

BLOOD ORANGE GRANITA

Serves 4

Blood orange granita is my take on an Italian ice. This is a simple mix of juice and sugar with a sweetness that almost hides the subtle surprise of the black pepper.

3½ cups (875 mL) blood orange juice
½ cup (125 mL) sugar
1½ Tbsp (22.5 mL) freshly ground black
   pepper (use a mortar and pestle)

Place all the ingredients in a bowl and whisk to incorporate. Pour the blood orange mixture into a large baking dish and place it, uncovered, in the freezer. Scrape it, crushing any lumps with a fork, every half hour until the blood orange granita freezes, approximately 1½ hours.

Remove the blood orange granita from the freezer and scrape with a fork to lighten its texture before serving.

AVOCADO PUDDING

Serves 4 (2 cups/500 mL of pudding)

Just blend it and let it set.

½ cup (125 mL) whole milk

1½ tsp (2.5 mL) gelatin (½ package gelatin)

1 ripe avocado

½ cup (125 mL) condensed milk

Zest and juice of 1 lemon

Pinch of salt

Place ¼ cup (60 mL) of the milk into a small bowl, sprinkle the gelatin overtop and stir to dissolve the gelatin.

Add the remaining ¼ cup (60 mL) milk to a small pot and warm it over low heat. Pour 1 Tbsp (15 mL) into the bowl with the milk and gelatin and stir. Pour this mixture into pot containing the warmed milk.

Place the remaining ingredients in a blender, add the warmed milk and gelatin and purée until smooth.

Divide evenly between four serving dishes. Place plastic wrap directly on the surface of the pudding to avoid a skin from forming and wrap tightly. Refrigerate for approximately 1 hour to set.

JAM PARCELS

Serves 4 (makes 24 parcels)

Jam parcels—I absolutely love these and making them gives me the same rush as making a stuffed pasta or wonton.

Vegetable oil for deep-frying

One 16 oz (454 g) package square wonton wrappers (usually about 30 in a package)

1 egg, whisked for egg wash

2 Tbsp (30 mL) raspberry jam

¼ cup (60 mL) icing sugar for dusting

Place the vegetable oil in a large pot, no more than one-third of the way up to prevent splashing or boiling over. Heat the oil to 350°F (175°C). Line a baking tray with three layers of paper towels.

Place the wonton wrappers on a clean, dry work surface and brush them with the egg wash. Place ¼ tsp (1 mL) of jam in the centre of each wonton, then gently lift the edges up and twist to create a parcel. Pinch tightly around the base to secure.

In batches, place the wontons in the heated oil to fry until golden brown. Once the wonton parcels are golden brown, about 2 minutes, remove them from the oil and place them on the paper towel to drain off any excess oil. Repeat this process with the remaining wontons.

The jam will turn into an oozing hot syrup, so please allow them to cool slightly before serving to prevent burning your mouth. Once the wonton jam parcels have cooled slightly, dust them with icing sugar and serve.

TAMARIND BALLS

Tamarind balls are just about mixing and rolling tamarind, sugar and your favourite hot sauce. They're failsafe and delicious—and it really is impossible to eat just one.

1¼ cups (310 mL) sugar

One 7 oz (200 g) package tamarind

1 Tbsp (15 mL) *sriracha* or Thai-style hot sauce

Pinch salt

Place ¼ cup (60 mL) of the sugar on a plate and set aside.

In a bowl, add the tamarind, *sriracha*, salt and remaining sugar and mix them together with your hands. Form the mixture into bite-size balls by rolling small amounts of it in your hands.

Roll the bite-size tamarind balls in the plated sugar. Enjoy.

PISTACHIO MACAROONS

Serves 4

Making **macaroons** is a fairly simple process: mix, dollop and cook.

1 Tbsp (15 mL) butter, softened

3 egg whites, room temperature

Pinch salt

Pinch cream of tartar

½ cup (125 mL) sugar

2 cups (500 mL) shredded sweetened coconut, toasted and cooled

1 cup (250 mL) unsalted pistachios, toasted and roughly ground in a food processor or mortar and pestle

Preheat the oven to 300°F (150°C).

Line a baking tray with parchment paper and grease it with the butter.

In a dry saucepan on medium heat, toast the coconut, just until it starts to turn light brown. Be careful not to let it burn.

Place the egg whites, salt and cream of tartar in a clean, dry mixing bowl at room temperature. Beat the egg whites until firm peaks start to form, then add the sugar slowly, continuing to whisk until they reach firm peak stage. Gently

fold the remaining ingredients into the egg whites, reserving ¼ cup (60 mL) of the pistachios for a garnish.

Place dollops of the mixture onto the prepared baking tray and sprinkle with the reserved pistachios.

Gently place the tray in the oven and bake until the macaroons are firm and lightly golden, approximately 20 to 30 minutes.

Remove the tray from the oven and place the pistachio macaroons on a cooling rack.

When you're hosting special events it's always great to create a unique cocktail for the occasion. There may be a theme or a concept behind the event, or the guests of honour may have a favourite taste or even a story that can be shared through a customized cocktail.

At the *Everyday Exotic* launch party we served two unique cocktails, one made with ginger beer and one with pomegranate. I drew from familiar ingredients and flavours that the crew had discovered when working on the show. Their faces lit up as they recognized the flavours and they began reminiscing about long days in the studio. Thankfully they remembered only the good times.

Rarely do you have to convince people to have a drink, but the customized cocktail is an excellent way to get a party started. It makes people feel special and it can be a conversation starter.

My advice when designing your own cocktails is to simply start with the flavours you like, whether you prefer sweet or bitter, cognac or vodka, alcohol or non-alcohol, bubbly or flat, lemon or orange or strawberry. Or customize your favourite tried and true cocktails—add a bit of ginger to your Manhattan, or guava to your Crantini. Give your customized cocktail a fun name and be sure to introduce it by name to your guests as you hand it out.

If you don't drink alcohol, you can just leave it out and get creative with textures, flavours, bubbles and colours.

The following pages contain some of my favourite drinks. They're a mix of light and refreshing and hearty and warming. All are full of flavour, can be made with or without alcohol and offer a creative alternative to straight-up soda pop and flavoured waters.

DRINKS

SPARKLING LIMEADE
Serves 4

1 cup (250 mL) sugar

1 cup (250 mL) water

4 sprigs of mint and 4 mint leaves
    for garnish

Zest of 1 lime

5 lime leaves, broken by hand

2 ripe plums, peeled, cored and roughly
    chopped

1 tsp (5 mL) salt

8 ice cubes

4 cups (1 L) cold sparkling water

Juice of 5 limes

Place the sugar and 1 cup (250 mL) water in a small pot, bring to a boil and remove from the heat. Add the mint sprigs, lime zest and lime leaves to the pot and allow to infuse for 30 minutes.

Strain the lime-mint simple syrup through a fine mesh sieve and place in the fridge to cool.

Place the plums and salt in a mortar and pestle and mash until they're roughly puréed. Then divide the plum mixture, reserved mint leaves and ice cubes between 4 tall glasses.

In a large measuring cup or pitcher, place the sparkling water, lime juice and the lime-mint simple syrup. Mix well and pour into the glasses.

WATERMELON TOWER
Serves 4

½ cup (125 mL) sugar, + 2 Tbsp (30 mL)
    to rim the glasses

½ cup (125 mL) water

½ bunch mint

8 cups (2 L) chopped watermelon

8 ice cubes

2 limes, 1 cut in half and juiced, 1 cut in
    quarters for garnish

Place the ½ cup (125 mL) sugar and water in a small pot, bring to a boil and remove from the heat. Add the mint to the pot and allow it to sit and infuse the syrup for approximately 15 minutes.

Allow the syrup to cool, then strain through a fine mesh sieve. Discard the mint and place the mint simple syrup in the fridge to cool.

Purée half of the watermelon in a blender with half the mint simple syrup and lime juice, then pour through a fine mesh strainer into a large pitcher. Repeat with the remaining chopped watermelon and mint simple syrup and place in the fridge until chilled.

Place the remaining 2 Tbsp (30 mL) sugar on a plate. Rim the tops of the glasses with a lime wedge and press the tops of the glasses into the sugar to garnish.

Add the ice cubes to the glasses. Pour the watermelon drink over the ice, garnish with the lime quarters and enjoy!

SWEET AND SOUR TAMARIND DRINK
Serves 4

6 cups (1.5 L) water

1 cup (250 mL) sugar

One 7 oz (200 g) package tamarind paste

1 whole star anise

1 cinnamon stick

Place all the ingredients in a pot. Bring to a boil and simmer for 20 minutes. Remove the pot from the heat. Strain the liquid into a pitcher through a fine mesh sieve and refrigerate.

Once cooled, divide the liquid between four chilled tumblers and serve.

WATERMELON TOWER

SWEET AND SOUR TAMARIND DRINK

SPARKLING LIMEADE

PASSION FRUIT MOJITO
Serves 4

8 sprigs of mint, leaves picked and torn
¼ cup (60 mL) sugar
Juice of 2 limes
4 oz tequila
2 cups (500 mL) ice
Seeds and pulp of 2 passion fruit

Place the mint, sugar, lime juice, tequila and ice in a cocktail shaker and shake well.

Divide the seeds and pulp of the passion fruit between four tall glasses. Pour the mojito mixture over the passion fruit and serve.

MANGO SANGRIA
Serves 4

4 cups (1 L) store-bought mango juice
2 cups (500 mL) dry white wine
2 mangoes, large dice
1 orange, cut into rounds
1 lemon, cut into rounds
2½ cups (625 mL) Prosecco
2 cups (500 mL) ice cubes

In a large pitcher, place the mango juice, white wine and fruit. Ideally, this should be left in the fridge to infuse overnight.

Pour the Prosecco and ice cubes into the pitcher just before serving.

CHILI HOT CHOCOLATE
Serves 4

7 cups (1.75 L) 2% milk
1 vanilla bean, split, seeds removed and reserved
1 long red chili pepper, split and seeds removed
1 Tbsp (15 mL) chili flakes
3 whole cloves
1 cinnamon stick
12 oz (360 g) dark chocolate, chopped
Pinch salt
1 cup (250 mL) 35% cream, whipped with 1 Tbsp (15 mL) sugar for garnish (or store-bought whipped cream)

Heat the milk in a large pot over medium-low heat. Add the vanilla seeds and pod, chili, chili flakes, cloves and cinnamon stick.

Stir the mixture with a wooden spoon, scraping the bottom and sides of the pot to ensure that the milk does not burn. Allow the ingredients to simmer for 15 minutes.

Strain the milk into another large pot through a fine mesh sieve and warm it over medium-low heat. Once the milk mixture is hot, add the chocolate in batches to the pot, whisking to incorporate.

Season with a pinch of salt.

Ladle the chili hot chocolate into four large mugs. Dollop the whipping cream overtop.

GINGER ICE CREAM FLOAT
Serves 4

4 cups (1 L) vanilla ice cream, softened
1 cup (250 mL) finely diced candied ginger
4 cups (1 L) ginger ale

Place the vanilla ice cream in a bowl. Add the diced candied ginger and fold to incorporate. Place the bowl in the freezer until the ice cream becomes firm.

Divide the candied ginger ice cream between four tall parfait glasses. Pour the ginger ale over the ice cream.

Serve with a straw and a long spoon.

PASSION FRUIT MOJITO

MANGO SANGRIA

CHILI HOT CHOCOLATE

GINGER ICE CREAM FLOAT

Acknowledgments

So many talented people have contributed to *Everyday Exotic* in so many different ways, and we would like to thank you all.

Food Network Canada for believing in us from day one. Tanya (famous last words—now go make a hit show), Leslie (you saw it from the beginning so clearly with your pinpoint vision—thank you for insisting on greatness and being great yourself), Emily, Karen, Kathy, Brynn, Muriel, Jaclyn, Cathy, Sarah, Stephanie, Anne Marie, Maureen, Barb, Christine, Jessica, Catherine, Lauren, Danielle and Zoi.

The entire *Everyday Exotic* crew—the fun of the show and this book comes from you all. Thank you for making it so much fun to come to work every day. Shelley (host is acting up, send in Shelley), Ben, Claudia, Justin, Toby, Susie, Simon, Joe, Denise, Jim, Miriam, Jessica, Alex, Phil, Russ, David, Mike, Andre, Ethan, Dominique, James, Angela, Travis, Alex, Neil, Marika, Jane, Peter, Elisa, Margaret, Gord, Amy, Rob, Pete, Julia, Matthew, Ross, Melissa, Vanessa, Bob, Doug and Ryan.

Our producers Toni and Steven who led this incredible team and grew the vision daily. You over-delivered.

Robert and his team at Whitecap for making this book real. Who knew one dinner so long ago would lead to this? I guess you did, Robert. Thanks for making a dream come true.

Joy and Jon, the hardworking team at Portfolio, for selling our show to such fine broadcasters around the world who have caught the *Everyday Exotic* bug. TLC SE Asia, New Zealand, Kuwait, Poland, America and the Caribbean.

Cooking Channel, Scripps and the Food Network for the madd love and support. Michael (Alberta represent), Bruce (you believed at FN and now at CC—thank you), Susie, Pat, Rhonda, Jeanne, Alison, Lauren, Kflip, Katie, Lynda, Lisa, Bryan, Jill and the entire kitchen team.

—*Roger and Al*

My wife and kids for putting up with my endless work schedule and standing by my side through every single moment. My parents, grandparents, siblings, extended family, nieces and nephews, in-laws and aunts and uncles, who have inspired and been part of so many of the memories and recipes you will find here. You are too many to mention individually but you all hold an individual place in my soul.

The big dog, Al Magee, for your support, belief and inspiration; so proud to be a speck in your world.

The other hosts I've had a pleasure to get to know, meet and become friends with. It is with a mix of admiration, inspiration and friendship for you all that I send this group hug.

My management, legal and accounting teams for their hard work and dedication to putting food in my family's mouths, watching my back and listening to my crazy thoughts. We appreciate it. Chris (let's do this), Greg, Cheryl, Ed, Krystal, Pam, Adam, Samantha, Brett and Terence.

—*Roger*

My wife, Melanie, for giving up the kitchen and moving all the kids into a hotel for two days so we could shoot the *Everyday Exotic* series demo and for all the support and good cooking throughout. Jake, John, Joseph and Stephen for seeing the world so purely.

To Roger, for opening up your life and your heart and sharing your unique passion for food and life so generously.

To my work family, Toni, Neil and Steven. Toni for keeping it all on track and for continuing to keep it all on track, Neil for keeping me on track and Steven for being on a track all your own.

To my benevolent twin, Glenn, and the team at Meridian Artists for keeping me busy and for so much generous and compassionate advice.

And to Clark and Mary, for giving me my first chance to produce a TV series and for so many years of good friendship and support.

—*Al*

Index